P9-EMD-954

Sensible Phonics

A SELF-TEACHING GUIDEBOOK

FOR TEACHERS

Thaddeus M. Trela
ED.D.

FEARON PUBLISHERS, INC.

BELMONT, CALIFORNIA

For Lou Burmeister

*and with appreciation to the many supportive
professors and students at The University of Texas
at El Paso*

ISBN-0-8224-6365-2

Library of Congress Catalog Card Number: 74-81750

Printed in the United States of America.

Contents

Self Quizzes

Inventory Tests for Pupils

Some First Words—A Preview

The goal of this handbook is to provide you with a practical learning guide to phonics, one that you can easily understand. It begins with explanations of what phonics is and how it fits into an intelligent program of helping students learn to read. Then comes the first of eleven self-help quizzes that give you a chance to see how well you are doing. Quite likely you'll enjoy these quizzes, for which answers are furnished after the last chapter.

Next, phonics generalizations are explored and the practical ones are identified (and listed in a single group at the end of Chapter 3). The Self Quizzes continue and should help you to remember those rules that are useful.

Clearing up the confusion in phonics "methods and materials" is the aim of Chapter 4. An explanation of the two basic phonics approaches, the several parts of a typical phonics lesson, and four ways of teaching phonics are some of the ideas presented. The information in this section intends a perspective about phonics that is probably as important as the phonics facts in themselves.

I am convinced, from classroom experience, that much difficulty can be avoided when there is a clear understanding of the terminology associated with phonics and word recognition. To help clarify the terminology, I have included in Chapter 5 a special vocabulary presentation in which terms used in phonics, structural analysis, and linguistics are explained simply and with examples. This glossary chapter includes four Self Quizzes that will promote your working knowledge of the necessary terms. Many terms are also explained in earlier chapters, of necessity, but they receive fuller treatment in Chapter 5. Since feeling comfortable with phonics terminology will help considerably in reading this handbook easily and working with phonics materials, you may wish to start with Chapter 5, even before you read Chapter 1. In any case, try yourself on the terminology in that chapter.

An inventory of phonics knowledge, with suggested directions and possibilities for testing use with pupils makes up the final part of the book. The inventory is a simple way to check any pupil's knowledge of phonics facts. It may be used also as an additional quiz for you to assess your own ability in phonics application.

A few further explanations are in order. You should be aware that a strict definition of phonics does not include information about syllables, roots, affixes, and stress in words. However, these topics and their concepts are included in various phonics workbooks, texts, and related materials. Hence they must be and are explained in this book to the extent appropriate.

The uncomplicated approach used in this book avoids getting involved in too many subtleties, details, and fine points. Only the current linguistic understandings useful for teachers are employed, so those who are intrigued by the history of language development and by fine linguistic discriminations should look elsewhere (and enjoy grappling with the present perplexities of linguistic relevancy).

But now, it's time to start—either with Chapter 1 or Chapter 5. As you begin, be assured that with a little effort you will gain a good basic understanding of what phonics is all about. Good luck! And I hope you enjoy this little book.

Thaddeus M. Trela

1 *Phonics in a Nutshell*

Phonics is a subject that is relatively easy to understand and master. However, so much has been said and written about phonics that it would not be surprising if you are a little puzzled or even apprehensive about it. What that one word—phonics—means may have been beclouded through its use in an inventive assortment of terms such as "phonovisual," "phonetic clues," and "phonic decoding." The idea behind phonics is very simple.

Basically, knowing phonics is knowing which speech sound goes with which written letter (symbol). Knowing that the letter *m* usually stands for the first sound we hear in m*an*, m*oney*, and m*other* is a phonics learning.

We can help children in learning to read by teaching them that the words they read are made up of letters that represent the sounds people make when they talk. Some letters more consistently represent particular sounds than do other letters. In using phonics as a teaching tool we are especially interested in these most consistent letter-sound "partners." The letter *d* is most often associated with the sound heard at the beginning of d*oll*, d*og*, and d*ay*, so this symbol-sound relationship is called *regular*. Knowing about such a dependable association can be helpful in learning to read. On the other hand, phonic associations having many exceptions are of little teaching value.

Many American-English words are completely consistent phonically; that is, the words are made up of letters, or letter combinations, that call set sounds to mind. In words such as *dig, not, run,* and *ham* the letters in each word call to mind a matching sound without much confusion. Such words are considered phonically consistent or regular.

Although many words are phonically regular, some are partly or even completely irregular because their letter parts do not stand for an expected sound. Pupils may have quite a bit of difficulty in calling to mind the sounds corresponding to the letters in words such as *eight, colonel, eye, genre, suede,* and *business.* Reading would be an easier skill to master if each letter were associated with just one sound. But such is not the case.

Now it may be interesting to try a pre-test of phonics regularity. Here is the first of a series of quizzes for you to try. In this quiz, you will try to determine which words are completely regular; that is, which words are entirely phonic in that the letters or their arrangement in a word agree with the expected, most consistent symbol-sound association. This self-quiz is an introduction to the series of quizzes in this handbook. However you do—and you may do better than you expect—don't despair.

Self Quiz 1

SOUND-SYMBOL REGULARITY

You are to indicate whether the 10 words in the list below are completely regular according to phonics. Circle the answer *yes* or *no* opposite each word, as is shown and explained in the two examples. (You need not write an explanation.)

The word	*Is the word completely regular according to phonics?*	
0. children	(yes)	no
00. been	yes	(no)

0. Yes, regular. The word's letter-sound correspondences agree with those that are regular.

00. No, irregular. Here the *ee* represents /i/; in a regular word like *beet* the *ee* represents /ē/.

1. me	yes	no
2. plan	yes	no
3. he	yes	no
4. one	yes	no
5. two	yes	no
6. three	yes	no
7. shimmer	yes	no
8. timely	yes	no
9. aisle	yes	no
10. phonics	yes	no

Answers follow Chapter 6.

2 *Phonics in Its Proper Place*

SEVERAL WAYS TO RECOGNIZE WORDS

Anyone who has worked with children or adults who are learning to read is continually surprised at the variety of avenues pupils take to accomplish the complicated reading task. Certainly there is not just one way.

Knowing phonic generalizations is a great help—perhaps the most important help—in learning to read, but it is not the entire or only avenue. We teachers must know the other ways of recognizing words—ways that are used with or instead of phonics—in order to have a more complete understanding to how we can help pupils to read. These other ways are discussed below.

SIGHT WORDS—MEMORY TYPE

Some words are best taught by rote, to be recognized at sight. An example, suitable for adults, is the word *chamois*. "Sounding out" the individual letters of *chamois* will probably not yield the correct /'sham-ē/ pronunciation.[1] An adult just remembers the word as a whole with little or no phonics. For beginning readers, words such as *two*, *Mrs.*, *eight*, and *eye* are usually taught as memory words to be recognized as wholes at sight.

---

[1] The symbols of the current Merriam-Webster dictionaries are used to indicate pronunciation. Thus *chamois* = /'sham-ē/.

Sight words are those words we recognize instantly as wholes. Other terms for sight words include *look-and-say words, memory words,* and *rote words.*

Seeing words in print a number of times and remembering them with a minimum of clues is a common adult way of learning to read new words. You will hear of people who deride the sight or look-and-say idea. But keep in mind that no one advocates that children—or anyone for that matter—memorize *all* words. Indeed, we often use a combination of helps to arrive at the correct reading of a word. Whatever method we use initially in recognizing a word, our goal is to make the word part of our sight vocabulary.

Some of our most often used simple words are not completely consistent in symbol-sound relationship. Children can be taught to use *some* phonic clues to read most of these irregular words but they must make considerable use of memory, much as they do for the multiplication tables (facts). This memorization is accomplished over an extended period of time and through many exposures to a word.

Reminder: Many of the most frequently used simple words are not completely regular phonically. Examples: *was, were, one, two, you, there, said, could, do, give, have, kind, of, to, mother, father, what, where, who, buy, know.*

Self Quiz 2

SIGHT WORDS—MEMORY TYPE

You are asked to indicate, in the following list, the words that may need to be learned as a sight word.

Selecting your answer requires you to determine whether the word's reading *completely* follows regular symbol-sound correspondences or whether it does not. A word like *bet* is easily read correctly because it has regular symbol-sound relationships; a word like *aisle* would be learned largely by sight, its letter sequence memorized, because the letters do not exactly correspond to the sounds these letters regularly symbolize. Thus *aisle* is a sight word.

Even if your phonics background is limited, you may be able to do quite well on this quiz, for it is akin to Quiz 1. Circle your chosen answer as the example shows.

The word	*Is the word to be learned by sight?*	
0. bayou	yes	no

0. Yes. The word needs to be learned by sight because its *ay* represents the sound /ī/ as in *bite*, not the /ā/ of *day*.

1. soldier	yes	no
2. brought	yes	no
3. friend	yes	no
4. once	yes	no
5. beauty	yes	no
6. go	yes	no
7. home	yes	no
8. smell	yes	no
9. women	yes	no
10. queen	yes	no

Answers follow Chapter 6.

SIGHT WORDS—CONFIGURATION TYPE

The word *Ypsilanti* (the name of a city in Michigan) is one that the author of this book immediately recognizes by its shape and look—its configuration. Perhaps you know the word *Yosemite* or *Mississippi* in the same way. We adults note words that are so unusual in their appearance we easily remember them. By guiding children to notice unusual features of a word we can help them to recognize it. Word shape may or may not go along with phonic help in learning a particular word.

It often surprises new teachers that children (as well as adults) have difficulty with common words (such as *should*, *and*, or *was*) yet easily remember a word like *grandfather* (probably their longest word), *rhinoceros* (peculiar and appealing), and *monkey* (it has a tail like one). Configuration can be a limited and temporary help in recognizing and remembering how to read a word.

Noting the peculiar qualities of words in shape, length, and unique inner features is called "using configuration to help read and remember a word." Examples: *neighbor* (length); *zigzag* (unusual); *radar* (it's the same backwards!).

　　Synonyms: Other terms for *configuration* are *word shape*, *word form*, and *word outline*.

Self Quiz 3

SIGHT WORDS—CONFIGURATION TYPE

In the list below, which words are unusual by reason of their configuration—so impressive visually that they may be recognized and remembered most easily because of unusual features? Circle your answer as in the example.

The word	*Has the word an unusual configuration?*	
0. some	yes	(no)

0. No. The shape is not unusual.

1. xenophobia	yes	no
2. ukulele	yes	no
3. tutti-frutti	yes	no
4. nerve	yes	no
5. around	yes	no
6. little	yes	no
7. teepee	yes	no
8. crevice	yes	no

| 9. grumpy | yes | no |
| 10. uses | yes | no |

Answers follow Chapter 6.

CONTEXT CLUES—WORDS

If we do not recognize a word instantly by sight, we may arrive at its pronunciation if the surrounding words indicate a word that fits. Using the sense of a passage to make an educated guess is called "using context clues." Along with memory, context clues often help adults to read accurately and with understanding. Children learning to read may also get help by using the clues of surrounding words along with phonics help. For example, the pupil who has never seen the word *mirror* may recognize it in the following sentence:

She looked at herself in the _____ on the wall.

Similarly, the number of possibilities is certainly narrowed in:

If only I knew what to give them for their _____! Now that they've been married this long they have everything!

It is important to remember that whatever method is used to recognize and read an unknown word, the strange word should be checked in its context situation to note if it makes sense.

Using the sense of the words surrounding an unknown word to help arrive at reading the new word is called "using context clues."

CONTEXT CLUES—PICTURES

The many illustrations in beginners' books also can help children to recognize words in the accompanying story. The combination of the picture help plus the surrounding words (and maybe a little phonics) may help the learner in making reasonable guesses of new and unknown words. Although pictures are fewer in schoolbooks above the primary grades, such extra visual impression can often continue to benefit slow-learning pupils and those from meager experience backgrounds. With direction, pupils can use these picture context clues effectively as temporary and supplementary help in reading unknown words.

STRUCTURAL ANALYSIS

"Sounding out" of all words letter by letter, especially long words, is an inefficient and awkward way of learning to read. Approaching a strange word by means of its *meaning units*[1] and *pronunciation units*[2] can help a student to recognize it. When a pupil looks to see how an unknown reading word is constructed, as by looking for root words or noting syllables, he is using structural analysis.

Structural analysis—sometimes called the twin of phonics—is an especially efficient method for students to use in recognizing (and understanding) many long words. Examples of words that lend themselves to structural analysis are:

> baseball, snowsuit (compound words)
>
> *un*appreciate, *re*do (words with prefixes)
>
> play*ing*, toast*er* (words with suffixes)

It should be noted that before a learner can analyze the structure of a word he must be able to recognize its parts. Structural analysis often depends upon phonic knowledge.

A pupil who can identify meaning parts (root and base words, prefixes, suffixes) and pronunciation parts (syllables) in reading words is using *structural analysis*.

Elementary structural analysis is often included as part of phonics teaching materials and programs. Therefore, this booklet includes terms that are associated with structural analysis, plus generalizations and background for the teacher. (See Chapter 5.)

DICTIONARIES

Even the best reader will encounter words that are difficult to recognize and may not be part of his meaning or speaking vocabulary. Children too, particularly by the third and fourth grades, meet words that are not part of their reading or speaking vocabulary and must deal with them independently. For these, a final help is the correct use of a dictionary.

Some words yield few phonic or other clues to correct pronunciation. Examples of such words are: *ewe, dough, toupee, soirée,* and *patois.* These

---

[1] See *morpheme* in Chapter 5.

[2] See *syllable* in Chapter 5.

demand a dictionary. In other situations, the learner may arrive at a tentative articulation of an unfamiliar word and will need to use a dictionary to be assured of the correct pronunciation.

A dictionary is the final "helping key" in recognizing and understanding words.

SUMMARY

Phonics is one of several avenues that a pupil can use to recognize unknown words. Along with phonics—and sometimes in place of it—teachers can guide students to become independent in reading by means of:

> sight or memory words
> configuration
> context word clues
> context picture clues
> structural analysis
> dictionaries

Important: Much unnecessary writing and argument about the place of phonics in learning to read has been heard for many years. Arguing about the place of phonics in reading instruction can be a waste of time. Today's teachers recognize the need for phonics instruction but today's teachers do not restrict themselves to phonics exclusively. Rather, teachers use phonics along with other reasonable and varied approaches which are appropriate to pupil and situation need.

Self Quiz 4

AIDS TO RECOGNIZING AND
PRONOUNCING WORDS

Which approach(es) is/are the simplest, most efficient, and most likely to be helpful in learning to recognize and remember the words in the list below? Choose from the following:

memory—sight
memory—configuration
phonics
structural analysis
context clues
dictionary

The word	The best approach(es)
0. jiggle	phonics—perhaps configuration
1. fancy	phonics
2. Xerxes	memory sight
3. team	S. Ph
4. conduct	S. A. P.
5. fleur-de-lys	P.
6. ultrafashionable	S. A.
7. headaches	C.
8. ought	M. C.
9. Cheyenne	Phonics
10. squeegee	S. M

Answers follow Chapter 6.

3 Especially Useful Phonics Generalizations

THREE IMPORTANT UNDERSTANDINGS

Great energy, money, time, and talent are expended in helping pupils learn to read—all in addition to the mental and physical efforts put forth by all the young Wandas and Willies over the land. As adults concerned with the learning of pupils, we want to make their efforts as efficient as possible. In our efforts to help students learn to read we should be informed of what is most practical in the teaching of phonics.

Teachers and their students need to keep in mind three important understandings. These are given below and then explained briefly afterwards.

1. English is a language in which phonics are not perfect; there is not a one-to-one correspondence of phonemes (sounds) and graphemes (letters).[1]

2. There are *some* phonics generalizations, or grapheme-phoneme (letter-sound) generalizations, that are very useful.

3. Flexibility in the use of phonics generalizations is necessary.

If English were a completely phonic language in which each letter would consistently stand for the same one sound, learning to read and write our language would be easier. Such, however, is not the situation. Our vocabulary has grown and continues to grow vigorously as we continue to ingest words from every part of the world. The constant addition has made English a very rich language in that there are more words and ways of expressing ideas in English than any other language.

---

[1] See *phoneme* and *grapheme* in Chapter 5.

We often take new words very much as we find them, keeping their original spelling and approximating their original pronunciation. Unlike the Russians—who have a supreme agency that periodically purifies the language of new nonphonetic word spellings—we have no language or spelling authority to rule on regularity and impose its rules on our speech and writing. (The French, at least, worry about all the English spellings creeping into their language.) Rather, every day we are adjusting our reading to new words spelled differently from the ways we might consider regular—some examples are *discotheque, psychedelic, cognoscenti, babushka, guru, junta.*

However, the grapheme-phoneme (letter-sound) correspondence in our language is not totally erratic. This second understanding is most important. There is enough consistency in the letter-sound association in English to formulate some useful generalizations that can help us in teaching reading.

There are very few letters or letter combinations that consistently represent just one sound; in other words, there are few phonics facts that are without exceptions.

In recent years a number of researchers have studied phonics in reading and have helped to derive a number of generalizations about the symbol-sound relationships. Many are very useful generalizations (some like to call them rules) that help in learning to read English. The question does come up as to what kind of phonics generalization is useful and what kind isn't. To be useful, should a generalization work 85 percent of the time? or 50 percent of the time? For our purposes here, the minimum for validity is 75 percent, a figure used by several of the researchers concerned with phonics generalizations. A 75-percent validity figure means that the generalization will work on *at least* three out of four words that present a spelling to which it may apply; or, said another way, if a pupil uses a rule on four possible words he can read three of them correctly. A generalization that is less than 75 percent effective is, of course, of more limited use.

Generalizations given in the following pages are at least 75 percent valid.[2] In addition, they are useful on many words, for care must be taken not to burden pupils with rules that apply to just a few English words. The generalizations here are not restricted to a few situations.

---

[2] See the end of this chapter for a list of useful phonics generalizations.

Flexibility in generalizing gives direction to the use of phonics in a total word-recognition program. Teachers must be always aware that in presenting ways of learning words they influence their pupils. The attitudes a teacher imparts become a part of the student and can serve or hinder the student's progress. A teacher may do considerable harm by filling the memory of a student with many absolute phonics rules as the only way of reading words. Reading clinics and remedial-reading teachers see a parade of learners who can recite phonics "rules" as they do the flag pledge—yet do not know how to apply the generalizations properly or how to combine them with other necessary helps. The author vividly remembers watching and hearing an eleven-year-old boy of above average ability laboriously trying to "sound out" the individual letters of the word *the* because it was the only method of word attack he knew. The pupil who does best in reading is not the one who is ready with a specific number of phonic rules, but rather the learner who can adjust to the variety of words with phonics knowledge *and* with other approaches.

Teachers are aware that some words must be memorized, many analyzed, and nearly all fitted into context; this same flexible outlook must be taught to the pupils. Except possibly in their beginning phonics lessons, pupils should work with all the necessary word-recognition skills at the same time; for example, they should sound out only as much of a word as is necessary to give them the pronunciation within the context of a sentence. More will be said about a flexible approach in a following chapter, which gives some phonics-teaching suggestions.

THANK GOODNESS FOR CONSONANTS

Although many consonant letters do represent more than one sound or can be "silent," most consonants in our language are very regular in that the individual or doubled consonant letters usually stand for one sound. The underlined consonant letters as they are used in example words below present the regular grapheme-phoneme relationship 90 percent of the times they appear in words.

boy	jam	nap	we
dad	keep	pad	zoo
farm	lad	rug	
hot	man	yet	

son—goes	ton—station	fix—exit
city—cat	giant—go	

Generalization: Consonant letters usually represent one sound.

But remember! There are few absolutes in letter-sound correspondence.
The letter *s* usually stands for sound /s/[3] heard in s̲un and the letter *t*
for the sound /t/ heard in t̲in. The second most common sound that *s*
represents is the sound /z/ in the middle or at the end of a word like *goe̲s*
or *pre̲sident*. The *s* pronounced /sh/ in *s̲ugar* and *s̲ure* is far less often
encountered. The second most frequent sound that *t* may represent is
the /sh/ heard in the middles of the words *nat̲ion* and *init̲ial*.

Generalization: After its most frequent sound, *s* next most often stands
for the sound /z/ in the middle or at the end of a word. After its most
frequent sound, *t* represents the sound /sh/ in the middle of a word.

Both the consonant letter *c* and the consonant letter *g* commonly
represent two sounds.
The *c* stands for the "soft" sound /s/ before the letters *e, i,* or *y* as in
c̲ent, c̲ivic, c̲ynic, suc̲cess; otherwise, *c* represents the "hard" sound /k/
as in c̲andy, atti̲c, c̲limb, civi̲c, cyni̲c, su̲ccess. This principle, like most
generalizations, is not absolute; but it is useful in about nine of any ten
c words.
The consonant letter *g* has the "soft" sound /j/ when it is followed
by *e, i,* or *y* as in the words *g̲em, g̲in, g̲ym.* Otherwise, *g* stands for the
"hard" sound /g/ as in the words *g̲o, do̲g, mu̲g, g̲as.* This principle is a
valid one to teach but a number of very common words taught early in
reading do not follow this rule. These exceptions include words such as
g̲irl, g̲et, g̲ive.

Generalization: The letters *c* and *g* when followed by *e, i,* or *y* usually
stand for their soft sounds; otherwise they represent their hard sounds.

Often taken for granted is the generalization that doubled consonant
letters—like *bb, mm,* etc.—represent a single sound. This guiding principle

---

[3] To distinguish them from alphabet letters, sound symbols are written or printed between
slant lines; *s* is a letter, whereas /s/ and /z/ are sound symbols. Although most sound symbols
are derived from alphabet letters, the sound symbols should not be confused with the letters.

is true most of the time in appropriate words: *pu*d̲d̲*ing*, *we*l̲l̲, *litt̲le*, *Ll̲oyd*. The chief exception is *cc* as in the words *ac̓cent*, *success*, and *accident*.

Generalization: Doubled consonant letters usually represent only one sound.

LETTERS—BUT NO SOUNDS

It is very difficult to formulate a generalization for letters that yield no speech sound, sometimes called "silent letters." A large number of words contain one or more letters that represent no sound but either are "silent" or else help form a familiar letter combination that represents only one sound. Teachers may wish to point out to pupils those that are more frequently encountered in reading, such as t̲ch (match), d̲g (fudge), w̲r (write), k̲n (know), and mb̲ (thumb). "Silent letters" exemplify the historical development of English spelling not keeping step with English pronunciation and are a fascinating study for intermediate and junior-high pupils.

CONSONANT DIGRAPHS[4]

In general, two-letter consonant combinations that stand for one sound (called digraphs) do just that—they represent one sound. But there is need for a degree of flexibility with respect to several often-read digraphs.

The digraphs *ng*, *ph*, and *ck* correspond to their customary sound almost all the time. The digraph *th* symbolizes only two sounds, one voiced (th̲*en*) and one not voiced (th̲*ink*). *Qu* has the blended sound /kw/ as in qu*ie̅t* most of the time and the digraph sound /k/ as in *techni*qu*e* far less o̅f̅ten. The consonant digraph *ch* most often stands for the /ch/ sound as in c̲herry, particularly in words used in beginning reading instruction. N̅ext, *ch* represents the /k/ sound as in *ec̲ho* or *ac̲he*, infrequently the /sh/ sound in the words *mac̲hine* or *c̲hef*. The digraph *wh* usually has the sound as heard in w̲h*at* (either /wät/ or hwät). Less frequently *wh* calls for the sound /h/ as heard in w̲h*ole*. The *nk* combination is really a blend of the digraph *ng* plus k but it o̅f̅ten appears as a digraph unit in phonics exercises.

---

[4] A review of the terms *consonant digraph* and *consonant blend* in Chapter 5 is strongly recommended.

Here is a list of consonant digraphs that is useful in phonics teaching:

si*ng*	*ph*oney	*th*in; *th*ese
ra*nk*	de*ck*	bou*qu*et; *qu*it
*sh*oe		*ch*at; *ch*orus
		*wh*en; *wh*o

Generalization: Consonant digraphs usually stand for one sound, although *qu*, *wh*, and *ch* sometimes represent other sounds.

Generalization: The consonant digraph *th* represents two sounds.

Self Quiz 5

CONSONANT GENERALIZATIONS

Do the graphemes (letters) *italicized* in the following word list conform to useful symbol-sound generalizations? In other words, do these consonant letters stand for their most common sounds? Circle your answers as the example shows.

The word and grapheme (s)	Does the grapheme stand for its most common sound?	
0. *ph*oto	⟨yes⟩	no

0. Yes. Here *ph* is a digraph and it does represent its most common sound, /f/.

1. *ch*ute	yes	no
2. *f*at	yes	no
3. par*t*ial	yes	no
4. *s*ound*s*	yes	no

5. go	yes	no
6. Jack	yes	no
7. why	yes	no
8. cynic	yes	no
9. matter	yes	no
10. sweetheart	yes	no

Answers follow Chapter 6.

THOSE TROUBLESOME VOWELS

Those who study our language write that American English contains between 19 and 22 common vowel sounds, depending upon how discriminating the particular linguist may be. These vowel sounds may be represented by a number of individual letters and letter combinations. In one substantial study, Ernest Horn found that 234 letters or letter combinations could be used to represent the 22 vowel sounds identified in English! There were 16 different spellings that would evoke the /ā/ sound that is called "long a." (The difficulty of working with the spelling of vowel sounds is a reason for one consonant-oriented reading method mentioned in the next chapter.)

This vowel complexity might seem serious enough to cause despair for the teacher and pupil. Fortunately, the situation is not entirely overwhelming. The majority of vowel sounds are what are often called the "long" and "short" sounds of the vowels. When you add the schwa—the "uh" or unaccented /ə/ sound—and the r-controlled vowels you have accounted for 90 percent of all vowel sounds.[5]

INDIVIDUAL VOWELS

The letters that are used individually and in combinations to represent vowel sounds are a, e, i, o, u, y, and w. The letter w is used in combinations only. The letters gh also are used infrequently in combinations with vowel letters to represent a vowel sound (example: sight).

Generalization: The letters a, e, i, o, u, y, and w are used alone and in combination to represent vowel sounds.

---

[5] See definitions of *schwa* and *controller consonant* in Chapter 5.

One surprise for new teachers noting spelling patterns is to find that the letter *y* represents a vowel sound far more often that it does a consonant. The letter *y*, when it represents a vowel, yields the short *i* /i/ sound most of the time within words, as in *hymn, synopsis*. At the ends of words, *y* is associated with the long *i* or long *e* sounds (*by, my, apply; lady, candy*).

(*Note:* Until recently some school dictionaries marked the *y* in multi-syllable words such as *pretty, baby,* and *sandy* as representing a short *i* sound.)

Generalization: The vowel *y* usually represents a short *i* sound in the middles of words and a long *i* or long *e* at the ends of words.

POSITION CLUES TO VOWEL SOUNDS

The position of single vowel letters in a word may give a clue to the sound of the vowel letter. Pupils may be encouraged to look beyond the vowel letter in a word to see if they can discover visual clues to the sound the letter will represent. A vowel sound that is in a word or syllable often may be determined by noting whether the vowel letter ends the word or syllable.

Open Syllable

If a single vowel letter ends a word, or ends a syllable within a word, we have an open syllable. Below are examples of open syllables. Note that an open syllable may be a complete word or part of a word.

me	hi	me-ter	do-nate
he	go	ta-ble	tri-fle
so	fly	sta-tion	mu-sic

The vowel letter in an open syllable is likely to have its own long sound about half of the time. In open one-syllable words (*be, my, no*) the vowel has its long sound most of the time, but there are relatively few such one-syllable words. However, the open-syllable generalization is useful in early reading instruction when the one-syllable words occur more often.

Closed Syllable

If a single vowel letter is followed by a consonant letter, the vowel sound that is represented may follow what is called the closed-syllable principle.

A closed syllable may be either a word or a syllable within a word, provided it ends with a consonant. Examples help to clarify what is meant by a closed syllable:

met	God	him-self	cat-nip
at	sun	nut-meg	at-tic

All the examples above include closed syllables—that is, each word or syllable ends in a consonant and the vowel letter has a short vowel sound.

Almost three of every four closed one-syllable words contain the short sound of the one vowel letter that is in the word. However, in the more numerous words of more than one syllable, only about two of every three closed syllables contain the short sound of the vowel.

We can see that the open- and closed-syllable principles generally do not meet the 75-percent utility figure. A working generalization that just about meets the criterion can be formulated by the inclusion of the "uh" schwa sounds[6] as alternative sounds in closed and open syllables of words of more than one syllable. Then the expanded generalization goes something like: "The vowel letter in an open syllable usually has its long sound or a schwa sound; the vowel letter in a closed syllable usually represents either its short sound or a schwa sound."

Examples of *closed* syllables that have schwa:

at-om	bal-lad	chick-en
	mor-bid	mi-nus

Examples of *open* syllables that have schwa:

a-go	ben-e-fit	po-lite

Generalization: In a closed syllable the vowel letter will most often represent its own short sound, less frequently a schwa sound; in an open syllable the vowel will most often have its own long sound, less often a schwa sound.

(*Note:* Teachers of beginning reading who work on many one-syllable words may wish to emphasize the short closed-syllable and long open-syllable sound patterns without any schwa complication.)

---

[6] See the definition of *schwa* in Chapter 5.

The generalization above will work on about three words in four that provide the applicable spelling pattern. Wording a generalization to make it effective on an even larger percentage of words lengthens and complicates the generalization considerably.

An understanding of the closed syllable is probably more important because (1) our language contains more short vowel sounds than long vowel sounds, (2) many beginning reading words contain short vowels, and (3) many series of school materials emphasize the short vowel sounds in the beginning stages of reading instruction.

FINAL VOWEL-CONSONANT-*E*

One of the most familiar and traditional phonics generalizations appearing in reading methodology materials relates to words like *bite* that end in vowel-consonant-silent-*e*. The rule states that the first vowel letter usually represents its long sound. For example, a pupil hesitates at the first vowel letter in *mine*, looks past a consonant, notices the final *e*, backtracks, and understands the vowel as a long *i*. The generalization does work about three out of four times when it can be applied, is thus legitimate to include in phonics instruction, and should be known by all teachers. It is most effective with the vowel letters *a*, *o*, *u*, and *y* and less effective with *i*-consonant-*e* and *e*-consonant-*e* words. Examples of appropriate words for the generalization include:

lone	these	case
	fine	use

Remember, very few phonics facts are without exception and this includes final vowel-consonant-*e*. The irregularities include common words such as *have* and *love* and longer words that end in unstressed syllables like -age, -ate, -ive, and -ine. A teacher helps pupils to understand and use phonics generalizations as less than absolute.

Generalization: In a word that ends in vowel-consonant-*e*, the final *e* represents no sound and the vowel letter will usually have its own long sound.

THE "STRONG" *R*

Many vowels appearing before the letter *r* will represent some other sound than the vowel letter's long or short sounds. What happens is that some vowel sounds are very difficult to say before the *r* and the vowel sound is often "colored" or affected, as we can read in words such as *bare, here, car, over, hurt, myrtle, worry.* (These are the "r-words" teachers may refer to.)

Often you will get something of a combined "uhr" sound for the vowel letter followed by *r*; examples of this schwa /ə/ sound are *collar, cover,* and *donor.*[7]

Generalization: A vowel before an *r* often represents a sound other than its long or short sounds.

ADJACENT VOWEL LETTERS OR VOWEL DIGRAPHS[8]

English contains many words spelled with two vowels side by side as in *please, lead, wait, may, see, school.* A useful rule helps to simplify the sounds represented by such adjacent vowel letters. Most such pairs represent one sound; in other words, they are vowel digraphs. Pupils may be taught that when two vowels are side-by-side they represent only one sound. Teachers may wish to remember that the chief exception to this guiding principle is the *ia* combination as in *tri-al, di-al, pli-able, gi-ant, pi-a-no.*

Generalization: Two vowel letters side by side usually represent one sound.

"Walking Vowels"

The sounds that adjacent vowel letters represent open wide the door to confusion unless a degree of care is taken. There is a well-known and much-used rule that "when two vowels go walking the first one does the talking," meaning that the first of the adjacent vowel letters represents its own long sound and the second vowel is silent. Examples: *boat, seat, toe, rain, street.* This "walking rule" is not to be trusted despite its pleasant ring and occasional applicability, for, unfortunately, it is true less than

---

[7] See Controller Consonant in Chapter 5 for a fuller discussion.

[8] See *vowel digraph* in Chapter 5.

half the time—as we read in s*ai*d, d*oe*s, br*ea*k, m*ea*nt, fr*ie*nd, r*ou*gh, thr*ou*gh. Though teachers should be aware of the "walking rule" because it may appear in teaching materials, they should realize its limited effectiveness.

There is no manageable rule that can be formulated to cover all, or even most, grapheme-phoneme relationships of adjacent vowel letters. But are there any suggestions in what to do?

Teachers may wish to lead learners to understand that flexibility is necessary in dealing with vowel-letter combinations and urge them to try the long and short sounds of the first and then the second letter of the vowel digraphs. The sounded result plus context may yield the correct reading.

Generalization: To recognize the sound that adjacent vowel letters represent requires a flexible approach—trying the long and short sounds of each letter plus examining context is a reasonable beginning.

Some teachers may find a more systematic and detailed approach preferable and may plan to teach particular generalizations to cover specific vowel-letter pairs. The most useful of these generalizations for specific combinations are given here:

1. The "walking rule" is most effective for vowel-letter pairs *ai*, *ay*, *ee*, *ea*, *oa*, and *ow*.

l*ai*d, afr*ai*d	str*ee*t, br*ee*d	l*oa*d, r*oa*d
st*ay*, pr*ay*	p*ea*ch, s*ea*t	sh*ow*, gr*ow*

Note: The *ea* often represents the short *e* sound as in *head, peasant*; *ow* also represents the diphthong /ou/ as in h*ow*, n*ow*.[9]

2. The *oi* and *oy* are different spellings of the same sound and usually represent the diphthong as in *oi*l and b*oy*.

3. The *ou* and *ow* represent the same diphthong, as seen in *ou*t and c*ow*. However, the *ou* most often represents the schwa sound heard in the often appearing suffix -*ous*, as in *enormous* and *tremendous*.

4. The digraph *oo* represents either the "long" sound, as heard in *food*, r*oo*m; or the "short" sound, as heard in l*oo*k, b*oo*k.

---

[9] See *diphthong* in Chapter 5.

5. The *au* and *aw* vowel digraphs represent the same sound, as heard in au*to* and a*w*ful.

6. The combination *ie* most often represents the long *e* sound as in bri*ef* and f*ie*ld or the long *i* sound as in d*ie* and p*ie*.

7. The vowel pairs *eu* and *ew* stand for the sound heard in the words f*eu*d and f*ew*; *ew* also yields the sound heard in br*ew* and cr*ew*.

8. The *ei* vowel pair most often represents a long *a* as in *ei*ght and fr*ei*ght; next, long *e* as in c*ei*ling; and less often short *i* as in for*ei*gn or long *i* as in s*ei*smic.

A teacher may also wish to point out to pupils that *io* and *ia* are used with *c*, *t*, or *s* to make up many suffixes that have the schwa sound. Examples: *action, musician, vision, martial*.

Students armed with the more useful generalizations and with a mental set that emphasizes flexibility eventually can master the grapheme-phoneme correspondences of the admittedly complex vowel-letter pair situation.

Self Quiz 6

VOWEL GENERALIZATIONS

Do the *italicized* vowel grapheme(s) follow useful letter-sound generalizations in the words below? If they do, circle *yes*; if they are exceptions to useful rules, circle *no*. (Grapheme = letter or letters that represent a sound.)

The word and grapheme(s)	Does the grapheme(s) follow useful sound-symbol generalizations?	
0. d*o*	yes	(no)

0. No. The open-syllable generalization does not work here. The *o* would have to have its long sound, as in *fo-cus*. This word represents an exception to the generalization.

1. st*a*-ble	yes	no
2. *i*n	yes	no
3. s*a*d-ly	yes	no

4. be-tw<u>ee</u>n   yes   no

5. g<u>oa</u>t   yes   no

6. a-g<u>ai</u>n   yes   no

7. n<u>ow</u>   yes   no

8. l<u>o</u>s<u>e</u>   yes   no

9. lemon-<u>a</u>d<u>e</u>   yes   no

10. <u>a</u>-gr<u>ee</u>   yes   no

Answers follow Chapter 6.

DIVIDING WORDS INTO SYLLABLES

A pupil who learns to separate words into syllables helps himself get clues to reading longer words. Analyzing the structure of a word into meaning units (morphemes)[10] and syllables in order to help say the word is not a word-analysis skill for a beginning pupil; neither is it completely established in the primary grades. Syllabic and morphemic analysis are especially needed throughout the middle grades and into high school, after many phonics learnings have become automatic for the student. (*Note:* Teachers should understand and pupils should be made aware of the difference between the way syllables are separated as they are heard in speech and the way words are divided into syllables in writing. For example, we hear and say /'spen-diŋ/, /'bil-diŋ/, but the dictionary and printers divide the words *spend-ing*, *build-ing*. Glossaries or small dictionaries may show only one kind of division.)

The number of single vowel letters or vowel digraphs is a clue to the number of syllables that a word contains. The chief exception to this is the silent *e* in words ending in vowel-consonant-*e*. Here are examples of how a pupil would be able to *visually* determine the number of syllables in words he is reading.

what	one single vowel letter seen, therefore one syllable
return	two single vowel letters seen, therefore two syllables
tree	one-vowel-letter combination (digraph) seen, therefore one syllable

---

[10] See *morpheme* in Chapter 5.

happy	two single vowel letters seen, therefore two syllables
happily	three single vowel letters, thus three syllables
like	*e* silent in final vowel-consonant-*e*; there-fore, as only one other vowel letter is seen, one syllable
flower, cradle[11]	two single vowel letters seen, two syllables
neighborhood	two vowel-letter combinations and one single vowel letter seen, thus three syllables

This guide doesn't always work—very few guides do!—but the generalization may help a pupil to read a word he doesn't already recognize in print.

Generalization: There are usually as many syllables in a word as there are vowel letters or vowel digraphs—excluding final *e* in vowel-consonant-*e*.

Of course, if a pupil already knows and recognizes the word he can easily determine the number of syllables by listening for the number of *heard* vowel sounds. This type of auditory discrimination may be helpful in spelling and in dividing words at the ends of written lines.

MEANING UNITS

Visual inspection of a word for its meaning units is a help in recognizing the syllables and it aids in reading a long word. These meaning units include prefixes, bases (roots), and suffixes. By looking for and recognizing meaning units that are already familiar, a pupil may often arrive at a correct reading and understanding of new words. Skill with meaning units can be a considerable help in reading new words throughout the school years and into adult life.

Base words are separate syllables; prefixes are almost always separate syllables, and suffixes are often separate syllables.

foot-ball	two base words
un-kind	prefix + base word
comfort-er	base word + suffix

---

[11] These words are examples of the growing number that are commonly said with fewer syllables than the spelling indicates—here one syllable: *cradle* = /'krādl/, *flower* = /'flaúr/. The two-syllable pronunciations are *cradle* = /'krād-ᵊl/, *flower* = /'flaú-ər/.

More intricate combinations than those given above are numerous. You will find all the terms associated with meaning units further explained the Chapter 5.

Generalization: Syllable division is usually made between meaning units, including prefixes, base (root) words, and suffixes.

Little Words in Big Words?

A somewhat distant cousin of meaning units may be mentioned in teaching materials and by teaching colleagues. This is the practice of finding "little words in big words" which may have some value in helping beginners in word analysis and can be effective as a partial clue in the reading of many words. For example, finding the known word *all* in the new word *tall* may be helpful for a beginner in reading the new word. But, the idea behind "little words in big words" does have the potential to confuse, as we can see in words such as *tallow, tally, allow,* and *pallid.* Further, there is no *he* in *the,* no *or* in *worry,* no *she* in *ashes.* It is probably more sensible to teach pupils, as soon as possible, to look for meaning parts such as prefixes, suffixes, and roots. Beginners, perhaps may be encouraged to merely try substituting different initial or final letters in words with spelling patterns that are similar; instances are *ball, hall, call, fall,* or *map, mat, man, mad.*

PHONIC/SYLLABICATION

Once a word has been divided into meaning parts—prefixes, suffixes, and roots—any further syllabic division is made by observing the way letters occur within the parts. And, just as awareness of meaning units can help a pupil in reading new words, knowledge of syllable division may aid him in approaching new words by systematic pieces.

In a word of more than one syllable the reader learns to divide unknown words between doubled consonants or between successive consonant letters, as in *sum-mer, win-dow.* Here care must be taken that consonant digraphs such as *ch, sh, ph,* and *th,* are not separated.

Examples: *sil-ver, cer-tain,* but *fa-ther* and *a-chieve.*

Generalization: When two vowel letters are separated by two consonant letters, usually divide the word between the consonants—but do not separate digraphs such as *sh, ch, ph,* and *th.*

What do we do when one consonant letter separates two vowels? With which syllable does the *t* in *mot̲or* go? Many teaching and workbook materials say that the consonant between two vowel letters should go with the second vowel. In a word like *water*, the separation is *wa-ter*. But this guide is not effective often enough to be efficient.

Pupils should understand that when one consonant letter separates two vowel letters some words will be divided before and some words after the consonant. The pupils should try reading a new two-syllable word first by dividing before the consonant letter. And, again, there must be care not to separate consonant digraphs like *sh*, *ph*, and *ch*. Here are examples of this generalization:

a-gainst

fa-ther

e-nough

ac-id

both-er

un-ion

Generalization: When two vowel letters are separated by one consonant letter or consonant digraph, divide the word either before or after the consonant or digraph. Try reading the word first with the syllable pause before the consonant.

An especially useful generalization directs syllable division of the many words ending in consonant-plus-*le*, like *ab̲le̲*, *eag̲le̲*, *ank̲le̲*, *puzz̲le̲*, *circ̲le̲*. The syllable division in such words is made before the consonant letter that accompanies the *le*. Said differently, *le* at the end of a word is rarely alone but is accompanied by the consonant letter in front of it.

han-dle

shin-gle

tre-ble

ar-ti-cle

Generalization: The consonant-plus-*le* is read as a separate syllable when at the end of the word.

TWO USEFUL STRESS PRINCIPLES[12]

After some exposure to phonics learning, a pupil may begin to look for visual clues to the stress within words. Knowledge of stress (or accent) grows in importance to the pupil as an increasing number of the words he encounters are made up of two or more syllables. In addition to being a possible help in reading a word, understanding of stress is helpful in using glossaries and dictionaries. Visual accent clues are emphasized in the later stages of word analysis.

Stress in English multisyllabic words tends to fall on syllables other than the last. In a two-syllable word like *'bod-y* the stress falls on the first syllable. In a word of three or more syllables, the greatest stress will tend to fall on one of the earlier syllables, not the last, as in the word *en-'thu-si-asm.*

Generalization: Stress in multisyllable words falls on an earlier syllable, not on the last syllable.

A major exception to the stress pattern given in the generalization above is the group of words that is made up of prefixes and root words. A second generalization takes care of such words as *de-'part, in-'deed, re-'turn.* Stress has a tendency to fall on root words rather than on prefixes, suffixes (derivational endings), and grammatical (inflectional) endings.[13]

Examples:

un-'do	prefix + base word
dis-'claim	prefix + base word
'dish-es	base word + inflectional ending
'box-ing	base word + inflectional ending
'ac-tion	base word + suffix
'quick-ly	base word + suffix

Generalization: The stress usually falls on or within the base word (root) in inflected or derived forms of words.

---

[12] See *stress* in Chapter 5.

[13] See *derivative* and *inflectional ending* in Chapter 5.

Self Quiz 7

APPLYING PHONICS GENERALIZATIONS

Phonics generalizations should be useful and reliable when applied to unfamiliar words. Since your vocabulary is much larger than a reading pupil's, only nonsense words will be unfamiliar to you. Accordingly, you will be confronted with five nonsense words to which you will apply the generalizations presented in this chapter. Assume that these words are entirely regular, that is, that they conform to phonics generalizations. And though artificial, they are constructed of real parts—phonemes and graphemes combined as they might be in real words.

Follow the directions. And be optimistic—you may do better than you expect.

    A. The nonsense word is *dackest*.

0. (*dack*)(*est*)   Circle the syllables.

0. Explanation: The word is separated after *ck*, *dack* evidently being the base word or root and therefore kept intact; *est* is an inflectional ending (as in *sweet-est*).

1. *d a c k e s t*   Circle the stressed syllable.

2. *d* in *dackest* has the sound of *d* in _____.

3. *a* in *dackest* is   short   long   schwa.   Circle the answer.

4. The *ck* has the sound of _____.

5. The *e* =   short   long   schwa.   Circle the answer.

6. *st* =   blend   digraph   diphthong.   Circle the answer.

    B. The nonsense word is *precynthir*.

7. *p r e c y n t h i r*   Circle the syllables.

8. *p r e c y n t h i r*   Circle the stressed syllable.

9. The *c* represents the sound of _____.

10. The *y* represents the sound of _____.

11. The *i* near the end of the word has the sound of _____ _____.

C. The two-syllable nonsense word is *goungle*.

12. *g o u n g l e*   Circle the syllables.

13. *g o u n g l e*   Circle the stressed syllable.

14. The first *g* in *gougle* is likely to have the sound of   *g* in *got*   *j* in *jot*.
Circle the answer.

15. The *ou* in *goungle* would have the sound of   long *o*   silent *u*
diphthong   schwa.   Circle the answer.

D. The nonsense word is *disrotion*.

16. *d i s r o t i o n*   Circle the syllables.

17. *d i s r o t i o n*   Circle the stressed syllable.

18. The sound of the first *o* in *disrotion* will be   long   short.   Circle
the answer.

19. The vowel sound of the *io* vowel pair in *disrotion* is most likely to
be   long *i*   short *i*   long *o*   schwa.   Circle the answer.

E. The nonsense word is *extome*.

20. *e x t o m e*   Circle the syllables.

21. *e x t o m e*   Circle the stressed syllable.

22. The *o* has the   long   short   schwa   sound.   Circle the answer.

F. Various nonsense words:

23. In the nonsense word *creds*, the *s* has the sound of _____
_____ .

24. The nonsense word *trayd* contains _____ (how many?)
syllables.

25. In the nonsense word *peedor*, the *ee* represents the sound of   short *e*
long *e*   schwa.   Circle the answer.

26. *s a t e r*   Circle the syllables.

Answers follow Chapter 6.

Self Quizzes 8, 9, 10, and 11 in Chapter 5 will provide much additional
practice with phonics terms and generalizations.

A LIST OF THE USEFUL GENERALIZATIONS

1. There are very few letters or letter combinations that consistently represent just one sound; in other words, there are few phonics facts that are without exceptions.

2. Consonant letters usually represent one sound.

3. After its most frequent sound, s next most often stands for the sound /z/ in the middle or at the end of a word. After its most frequent sound, t represents the sound /sh/ in the middle of a word.

4. The letters c and g when followed by e, i, or y usually stand for their soft sounds; otherwise they represent their hard sounds.

5. Doubled consonant letters usually represent only one sound.

6. Consonant digraphs usually stand for one sound, although qu, wh, and ch sometimes represent other sounds.

7. The consonant digraph th represents two sounds.

8. The letters a, e, i, o, u, y, and w are used alone and in combinations to represent vowel sounds.

9. The vowel letter y usually represents a short i sound in the middles of words and a long i or long e at the ends of words.

10. In a closed syllable the vowel letter will most often represent its own short sound, less frequently a schwa sound; in an open syllable the vowel will most often have its own long sound or, less often, a schwa sound.

11. In a word that ends in vowel-consonant-e, the final e represents no sound and the vowel letter will usually have its own long sound.

12. A vowel before an /r/ often represents a sound other than its long or short sound.

13. Two vowel letters side by side usually represent one sound.

14. To recognize the sound that adjacent vowel letters represent requires a flexible approach—trying the long and short sounds of each letter plus examining context is a reasonable beginning.

15. There are usually as many syllables in a word as there are vowel letters or vowel digraphs—excluding final e in vowel-consonant-e.

16. Syllable division is usually made between meaning units, including prefixes, base (root) words, and suffixes.

17. When two vowel letters are separated by two consonant letters, usually divide the word between the consonants—but do not separate digraphs such as sh, ch, ph, and th.

18. When two vowel letters are separated by one consonant letter or consonant digraph, divide either before or after the consonant or digraphs. Try reading the word first with the syllable pause before the consonant.

19. The consonant-plus-*le* is read as a separate syllable when at the end of a word.

20. Stress in multisyllable words usually falls on an earlier syllable, not on the last syllable.

21. The stress usually falls on or within the base (root) word in inflected or derived forms of words.

REFERENCES

The author is indebted to Lou E. Burmeister for her generosity in sharing her work in word-analysis generalizations. Much of Professor Burmeister's research, and that of the author's, is based upon:

Hanna, P. R., Jean S. Hanna, R. G. Hodges, and E. H. Rudorf, *Phoneme-grapheme Correspondences as Cues to Spelling Improvement*, Washington, D.C.: Office of Education, Department of Health, Education, and Welfare, 1966.

Other published sources that influenced the generalizations used in this booklet are:

Burmeister, Lou E., "Content of a Phonics Program Based on Particularly Useful Generalizations," in *Reading Methods and Teacher Improvement*, N. B. Smith, editor. Newark, Delaware: International Reading Association, 1971, pp. 27–39.

Clymer, T. L., "The Utility of Phonic Generalizations in the Primary Grades." *The Reading Teacher*, 1963, 16: 252–258.

4 *Phonics Methods and Materials— Some Suggestions*

The available phonics methods and the published materials that accompany them can appear overwhelming. The steady outpouring of materials with fascinating names and promises has increased in recent years. Such words or phrases as "linguistically oriented," "creative," "dynamic decoding," "phonic color cues," "discovery," and "perceptual phonic keys" attempt to convince the interested teacher that a particular method or group of materials is modern, different, exciting, and better than anything else on the market.

This entire area of phonics instruction and materials requires of the teacher a determined effort to maintain a judgment based on experience and research evidence. All too often we have read and seen emotional testimonials and phonics instruction based on the energetic personality of an individual rather than on experimental study and trial.

Are there any guidelines?

Yes, there are some that those interested in practical phonics instruction should consider. An awareness of the evidence, practices, and understandings discussed below may help in approaching phonics instruction and materials with more reason than passion.

ONLY TWO FUNDAMENTAL APPROACHES

It is probably surprising to realize that the basic phonics approaches simply come down to two—the synthetic and analytic methods. It is worth the time and effort to understand these two terms in their use with phonics. Once you understand, for example, what a synthetic approach is, you can recognize the approach however it is presented.

The Synthetic Approach to Phonics

A phonics system is using the synthetic approach if it begins with attention to individual letter names or individual sounds and then proceeds to blend these individual parts together to arrive at the reading of the word. The synthetic approach begins with the individual units—letters or sounds—and puts these together to form words. For example, the teacher who tells the pupil that

$$\text{“buh” + “a” + “tuh”} = /\text{bat}/$$

is using synthetic phonics. And the teacher who says that

$$bee + ay + tee = /\text{bat}/$$

is also using a synthetic approach, in this case employing the letter names.

In synthetic phonics, pupils are often taught the individual sounds that go with the letters and then are asked to put these sounds together to approximate the word:

$$/\text{m}/ + /\bar{\text{e}}/ = /\text{m}\bar{\text{e}}/ = \text{me}$$
$$/\text{g}/ + /\bar{\text{o}}/ = /\text{g}\bar{\text{o}}/ = \text{go}$$
$$/\text{f}/ + /\text{r}/ + /\bar{\text{e}}/ = /\text{fr}\bar{\text{e}}/ = \text{free}$$

Here is the way a teacher might use synthetic technique:

Print the word *let* on the board. Point to the opening letter *l*. Say: "This is the letter *l*; it makes the sound /l/. The next letter is the letter *e*; it makes the sound /e/. The next letter is the letter *t*; it makes the sound /t/." Have the child repeat the separate sounds after you as you make them; then have the child try the entire word sound by sound; then blend the different sounds into the whole word until it is a unified, complete word. Repeat the word for the child with exaggerated sound stresses, making short pauses between the three sound elements. Ask the child to listen closely to the sounds as you point to the particular part of the word being sounded. Then ask the child to say the word.

Note: In the example given above the teacher will not exaggerate the vowel or "uh" part of the sound with the consonants; and the teacher may be fully aware that letters do not "make" sounds but find the expression useful temporary terminology.

The Analytic Approach to Phonics

In analytic approaches the teacher begins with the complete word and then leads the pupil to investigate the parts that make up that word. Said another way, analytic phonics begins with words a student already knows as wholes and then helps him to discover that these whole words are made up of separate sounds and letters.

Many basal reading-instruction systems use analytic phonics in that they begin by teaching a number of words to pupils as wholes by numerous exposures. The pupils memorize the words without thinking about the word parts. When several of these known words have a similar phonic symbol-sound association, that phonics understanding is taught. An example may help explain the analytic method.

Write on the board a column of words all of which begin with the letter *b* and all of which the pupils already know by sight as wholes.

boy

big

band

baby

ball

The teacher can either read the words aloud or ask the pupils to read them. As the words are read, the students are asked to listen to the sound heard at the beginning of each word. The initial /b/ sound is emphasized but not distorted. The pupils are then invited to read the words in unison, listening carefully to the sound /b/ as they say the words. The pupils are asked to look at the words carefully and name the letter that begins each word. They are encouraged to supply other words which begin with the sound /b/ as heard in the list of words. Usually the students would not be asked to isolate the sound or the letter *b* as "buh" (although a little of this may be done if it is found to be helpful). It is considered best that pupils should hear the sound /b/ as it occurs in words.

The following arrangement may help in differentiating between the analytic and synthetic approaches:

	Begin with	*End with*
Synthetic	Letter sounds *or* Letter names	Word Word
Analytic	Word Word	Letter sounds *or* Letter names

Which approach is best? Variations of both are used successfully and four techniques are exemplified later in this chapter.

THE FOUR PARTS IN A PHONICS LESSON

When stripped to the bare essentials, every—or almost every—phonics lesson may be said to have four necessary parts or steps. These four parts are visual discrimination, auditory discrimination, blending, and contextual application.

Being able to see differences between letters (visual discrimination) and to hear differences in the sounds that make up words (auditory discrimination)[1] are obvious requisites for conducting any phonics lesson. That pupils really do see and hear differences is always checked in phonics instruction. (Note: This checking is not simple. For example, try checking a number of adults to discover whether they hear the differences in the vowel sounds of the words *pin* and *pen*.)

A third necessary step—sometimes difficult for some pupils—is the blending of the individual sounds to make up a word in the synthetic approach or the substituting of letters to make up different words (substitute *r* for the *p* in p*ot* to make r*ot*) in the analytic approach. Blending is done easily enough by most pupils but can be a serious problem for a number of students, requiring considerable attention, variety of practice, and much patience on the part of teachers.

The fourth and final step is to test the word in context. This may not be absolutely necessary each time but it is a wise idea because it is an applied check of the new learning and because some spellings have different readings in different context, such as *live*, *wind*, *lead*, and *read*.

Two brief examples of the parts of a phonic lesson:

---

[1] See *visual discrimination* and *auditory discrimination* in Chapter 5.

At the first-grade teacher's side, Jeff was receiving individual attention for oral reading. In a final paragraph he confused two words: "The children were now in the middle of all the tall (fall) leaves. The fall (tall) trees were covered in colors of brown, yellow, and red."

The teacher isolated the two words *tall* and *fall* and asked him to note the difference in the beginning letters (visual discrimination). She asked him to say the words carefully after her and note the difference in the beginning sound of the two spoken words (auditory discrimination). Jeff was asked to find examples of either of the words in the story as the teacher pronounced them. The teacher then printed the last three letters ___*all* and tried adding and erasing *t*'s and *f*'s and asking Jeff to read each completed word (blending).

The paragraph was re-read to make certain the words were read correctly and a couple of teacher questions made certain the words were understood in the sense of the writing (contextual application).

Hannah balked completely and looked puzzled at the word *hostel* in reading a sentence of a newspaper feature story that a junior-high teacher was using as a basis for individual conference instruction. The sentence was: "The girls, travelling in Austria, agreed they did not like the hostel atmosphere."

"That's a good word for a hiker and camper like you to know, Hannah," the alert teacher said. "Take a close look at the word and divide it into two parts. . . . Say those two parts: /häs . . . təl/. . . . Now put the two parts together and say them naturally: /'häs-t°l/. And this story has a glossary at the bottom of this page. Find *hostel* and see what it means. . . . Now try reading that sentence again. . . . And just to make certain you remember that word, use it in a sentence of your own for me."

PHONICS IN BASAL READERS

The graded anthologies—stories, plays, poems, etc.—that are used almost universally in some way for reading instruction in schools are commonly called *basal readers*, but there are other names including *pupil core books*. The teacher's editions of each basal reader includes the literary material to be read by pupils plus lesson plans which suggest ways that the reading material may be used to help pupils learn how to read and to improve their present reading skills. Accordingly, the teacher uses the selections in the basic or core reader as a means through which the many skills and abilities of reading are practiced. A reading of the teacher's manual for the basal reader reveals the relative emphasis of phonics in the reading program.

The phonics emphasis in the teacher manuals of the most widely used basal reader series (or "systems") usually begins in the first-grade or later-kindergarten materials and is heaviest in the grade-two and grade-three materials. Dictionary skills often receive special attention in the latter part of grade three and in grade four. Structural-analysis skills become progressively more complicated and mature through the grades. Although most teaching materials use the word phonics, you may encounter "letter-sound relationships" instead.

Today's basal reading programs include adequate phonics programs for most learners. Critics who claim there is little or no phonics emphasis in basal reading systems often have not looked at the indexes, the tables of contents, or the individual lesson plans and exercises of *today's* materials. Even a cursory look through a second-grade teacher's edition of a current core reader may be something of a surprise to those who have been away from teaching or schools for just a few years.

The point is—whatever basal readers of the past were like—that most of today's readers contain a wealth of phonics instruction. And a personal examination of an up-to-date basal reading program is advised before accepting added-on phonics materials and extra periods of instruction.

IS AN ADDITIONAL PHONICS PERIOD NECESSARY?

There are individual teachers and entire school districts that schedule extra, separate phonics periods to supplement the reading period. One pattern finds the additional phonics period of time scheduled for the afternoon with the reading program in the morning.

The practice of having separate periods for phonics instruction disturbs many who are interested in a practical reading program on several grounds. The time is needed for other important studies, and separation of phonics from reading instruction is an artificial situation. Perhaps the most important reason for concern about additional phonics time is in the accumulated teacher experience and research evidence which indicate that extra phonics periods are not necessary if the regular reading period is efficiently used by teachers.

Over 25 years ago the investigations of Paul E. Sparks and Leo C. Fay seriously questioned the value of supplementary phonics instruction. What such studies are saying is simply that if children receive planned, sequential reading instruction, such as they may receive in a well-done basic reading program, *most* of them do not need extra phonics work. Rather than having extra periods of phonics for everyone, it makes more sense to have extra reading-instruction time for those who need such extra work. Their needed extra instruction may not be in phonics. Pupils may need strengthening in, for example, oral reading, careful silent reading, developing a larger sight vocabulary, dictionary exercises, and comprehension skills.

Many of us probably remember long sessions of studying what we already knew—for instance copying all spelling words ten times each, even those we knew very well how to spell! Recently, the author watched daily required 15-minute phonics reviews recited by all in an average-ability sixth-grade classroom in a large western city. With practical use of time in mind, teachers would do well to include solid phonics instruction as an integral part of their regular reading-instruction periods and to use any extra reading time discerningly according to the special needs of individual children or particular groups of pupils.

THE BEST PHONICS PROGRAM

Phonics methods and materials abound. Almost all publishers of reading-instruction materials include workbooks, games, sets of prepared ditto masters, word-card arrangements, film strips—and much more—in their catalogs, available separately or combined in "kits," "laboratories," "programs," and "systems." It might be comfortable to know which set of materials and which approach is the best, but common sense and experience quickly demonstrate that there is no "best."

Just as there is no one way that is best for teaching all pupils how to read—or how to do almost anything for that matter—so there is no one set of phonics materials or one way of using them that is superior for all learners.

Considerable prudence is required of teachers in the face of dynamic personalities and /or colorful, elaborate, novel materials that superabound and can arrive in an exciting flurry of promise as "the answer to all your reading problems."

Whatever the sincerity and energy of a number of active promoters of personal phonic "systems" or however logical, modern and slick some newer materials may be, this fact remains: There is no hard evidence that any one phonics program is consistently best for all learners.

And where does this leave the teacher? As we can see again and again, methods and materials must be appropriate to the natures, needs, and interests of the individual teachers and of the pupils that teachers work with. It may well be that many teachers will find the phonics programs in the series of a basic reading program adequate and suitable to their classrooms. Others may need to supplement their core program with practice materials such as phonics workbooks; some may want to modify the basal approach by judiciously omitting unneeded repetition for fast learners; still others may wish to motivate interest in phonics through learning-game situations or through interesting new phonics materials. Accordingly, the "best" comes down to individual teachers helping their pupils learn according to the individual personal characteristics of the teachers and their learners.

THE NEED FOR FLEXIBILITY

We have gained considerable perspective about phonics from past research studies and teacher experience. New information, materials, and methods, however, continue to come forward to challenge some of our favored attitudes and practices. Linguistic applications are only beginning to be translated currently into usable ways and means; "open" classrooms, programmed instruction and individual contract-plan study arrangements are innovations being tested; dictionaries are changing, with every new edition reflecting current vocabulary and speech patterns. As teaching techniques and supplies evolve in our dynamic society, so attitudes and approaches toward phonics must be constantly updated.

A practical approach to phonics instructions is, of necessity, a flexible one. "Flexible" here means adaptable, helpful, realistic. Instructors still refusing to accept the schwa sound may appeal to "old-fashioned standards," but they are simply out of date. Teachers exclusively searching for "little words in big words" and ignoring meaning units (morphemes) are not only old-fashioned, but in addition may do their pupils a disservice. Phonics materials or procedures that depend upon hundreds of rules are not only dull but worse—not in keeping with effective learning practices; teachers clutching well-worn sheaves of phonics worksheets may claim they have *the* answer to the teaching of reading but cold, unemotional evidence shows them less than foolproof.

Teachers, parents, and pupils are united in their desire for finding a simple, quick, economical way to learn to read. But, as this book insists, there is no one, clear-cut, by-the-numbers easy way. Approaching phonics and the teaching of reading flexibly is the only honest, realistic way.

The flexible teacher uses several methods to help his charges learn to read well and knows that different methods are effective with different pupils: that Hannah learns words best by writing them; that Elaine learns by saying the words distinctly while her finger slides under the letters that spell them; that Neil and Bill have grasped and remembered several words (*through, over, under, on, in*) by acting them out and immediately "framing" with their hands the written words on the chalkboard. Such an adaptable approach, of course, is more difficult for the teacher than a rigid one-book, one-method, one-set-of-rules, one-attitude, one-standard approach.

Do these questions tell something about a teacher?

> That doesn't sound right, does it, Craig? Try saying the word another way.

> Frances, why do you say that's a funny-looking word?

> Ella, did that word make sense in the sentence about what cats eat?

> Now do you think we can remember our two new words? Close your eyes. Can you see one of them on your mental TV's? Is the picture of the first one clear? . . . Writing them down can help us to remember how to say them. Say the sounds to yourself as you write them.

> Dick and Paul are today's word detectives and will show us the new words in the dictionary.

> Yes, Tony, that word has an *r* in it—now try to read it again.

> Put your reading card over the first three-letter prefix—you know that word—fine! Now add the ending to it.

> And when you're finished you can review saying your word cards with your partner.

> Almost all words fit our rule, but not quite all—so let's try it another way.

Comments such as those above are made daily in classrooms and by helpful parents in the course of helping children read and remember words. A varied approach attuned to individual children is not only the practical way but moreover is the way that helps children to gain a flexibility in approaching words—they have more than one way to "attack" the strange word!

FOUR WAYS OF TEACHING PHONICS

The ways of teaching symbol-sound correspondence are many. Probably the best technique for teaching phonics is the one that is suggested by the materials at hand—basal series, phonics workbook, or word-game laboratory kit. Four phonics-teaching techniques are described below and may be used as alternate methods or for the purpose of variety.

Single-Letter Phonics

Learning the sounds that are represented by letters and blending these individual sounds together to approximate words is the heart of the single-letter (synthetic) phonics approach. Pupils would begin with the more regular letter correspondences to consonant sounds and to short vowel sounds in one-syllable words. The consonant variations and long vowel sounds would follow as soon as possible.

The idea is to have the pupil *mentally* blend the individual sounds of a word before he says the word. In a word such as *get*, the pupil *thinks* the individual sounds of /g/ /e/ /t/ that he knows and tries to put the three sounds together without any /uh/ sounds between them. So the pupils would not say "guh . . . eh . . . tuh" but would reason out the three letter sounds to come near the pronounced sound of the word *get*. Advocates of this sound-blending system say that a pupil does not need an exact pronunciation of a word, but rather an approximation, because he almost always knows orally the word he cannot read. All the student needs is a crude blending operation to bring him close to the accurate pronunciation; this approximation, combined with context clues, will help him read the word.

Supporters of the system say that sound blending should not be dismissed merely because it is not suitable for all words. Sound blending, advocates say, makes it possible to greatly lessen the number of words a student has to memorize. The method is suggested for slow learners, for those who can't memorize words as wholes, and for pupils who cannot put phonics generalizations into personal practice. Many remedial reading teachers find the synthetic single-letter approach effective. William Kottmeyer, school administrator and author, who is identified with the reading-improvement program of the schools in St. Louis, Missouri, is a strong advocate of single-letter phonics in his *Teacher's Guide for Remedial Reading* (Webster Publishing Company).

Discovery Phonics

The phonics approach probably most approved by those in the reading forefront is what is today termed phonics by discovery. It is an analytical approach and is a current name for learning phonics via the inductive method. The analytical approach has been explained earlier in this chapter.

Discovery phonics tries to get the pupil to perceive for himself some generalizations about symbol-sound relationships rather than have rules told to him directly. A teacher guides a student to examine what he knows or what he is learning and leads the student to arrive personally at new understandings.

A simple example dealing with the sound represented by the letter *y* in one-syllable words demonstrates the method.

On the chalkboard the teacher writes several words that the pupils have already encountered and know:

by

my

cry

try

The teacher then leads the students to note the recurring sound at the ends of these known words. Very likely, the pupils will note that the *y* letter alone at the end of (one-syllable) words represents the long /ī/ sound. With this understanding elicited, the teacher may write on the chalkboard several words that have not yet been met in the reading program—"new words":

dry

fry

shy

spy

pry

"Now that we know the *y* at the end of a short word stands for the long /ī/ sound, I'll bet we can easily read these words." The words are read aloud and their meanings noted.

Sometimes a teacher may ask the pupils for other words that "end the same way" (with a *y*) and write the suggested words on the chalkboard. However, this may become awkward *if* students are disturbed when you reject inappropriate suggestions (in this situation, examples such as *die, rye, lie*, etc.).

The discovery approach can be used in almost all areas of word study, including structural analysis and accent. A more advanced example follows:

A teacher puts known words on the chalkboard, then asks the question: "Where is the accent in each word?"

pronunciation

association

action

station

deception

The discovery is soon made that the strongest stress falls on the syllable before the *tion*. "Let's test this understanding," says the teacher. The testing may then be done in a number of ways, such as having other suitable words said orally, writing words down on paper or on the chalkboard and trying them out together or individually, or looking in the dictionary. The teacher may want to end the lesson by trying words that have not been met or are likely to be long and difficult to pronounce.

Minimum Phonics—Consonants Plus Context

A third technique directs a pupil to use the minimum of sound clues plus context help in order to read a word which is usually found to be familiar when spoken. This method considers consonant letter-sound associations largely invariable and vowel letter-sound associations generally unreliable and usually unnecessary. Therefore, a child is asked to use a minimum of sounding help—consonant letter sounds—plus context sense to unlock a strange reading word which he already knows as a spoken word.

An example demonstrates how this technique might work.

We sailed our boats on the _____ in the park.

Perhaps the word is *pond, basin, reservoir?* But let us notice the first consonant and see what happens.

We sailed our boats on the l ____ in the park.

Now the word possibilities are considerably lessened. But let's go on the next consonant.

We sailed our boats on the l–g____ in the park.

Aha! It must be *lagoon!*

Note how this method works in sentence examples below with either all or just some of the consonants indicated in selected words:

> He likes his pet c–t.
> His l–g hurt.
> John put his –rm around his friend.
> Tom t– –k his wagon home.
> Please st– – running!
> Slice the br– – –.

It is apparent that a pupil has to know the sounds most commonly represented by the consonant letters and consonant digraphs to use this technique. An average oral vocabulary is also necessary. And the goal is a minimum of confusion and sounding effort on the part of the pupil. But, as with all ideas, teachers reading this book may wish to adapt or modify the technique for their own word-analysis program rather than depend upon it completely.

Make It a Game!

For symbol-sound associations to become established, a pupil requires many exposures to each pattern. But repeating rules or workbook exercises over and over is about as interesting to a pupil as washing dishes or shaving are to most adults (or grading papers is for a teacher). We adults often turn a very routine task to a kind of game—against time, with a new procedural twist, accompanied by rhythmic strokes, or whatever.

Even more than an adult faces an unweeded garden as a warrior rooting out the invading foe, a student needs game-like situations to help his phonics learning along. Hence the maxim: Make it a game!

Most basal readers have games built into their suggested daily lesson plans; the teacher need only establish or introduce the spirit of a game situation. A letter or request to the book representative for the publisher of the basal reading series often yields free pamphlets devoted to game activities.

Teachers who want ideas for phonics games can get them easily through the widely available periodicals *Grade Teacher* and *Instructor*. Also, a considerable number of inexpensive game-book resources are available, including these two

Reading Games. 1960. The Educational Publishing Company. Darien, Connecticut 06820.

Reading Aids through the Grades. 1951. Teachers College Press, Teachers College, Columbia University, 1234 Amsterdam Avenue, New York, N.Y. 10027.

An excellent source that contains many useful game ideas is Chapter 5 in *Improved Reading through Individualized Correction*, second edition. 1968. By D. G. Schubert and T. L. Torgerson. William C. Brown Company, Dubuque, Iowa 52001.

A forthcoming revision is titled *Improving the Reading Program*.

Commercially prepared game kits may offer another choice. Here are three examples:

Phonics We Use Games Kit. Lyons and Carnahan, 407 East 25th Street, Chicago, Illinois 60616. Ten games.

Get Set: Games for Beginning Readers. A boxed collection.

Linguistic Block Series. Scott, Foresman and Company, 1900 East Lake Avenue, Glenview, Illinois 60025.

Many teachers like to create their own games or to adapt old favorite games like bingo to suit their phonics purposes. Teachers often have their pupils help construct such aids as word wheels, flash cards, and "rolling cubes" (dice!).

Some cautions should be made about games. Teachers (and parents) should avoid using too many of the conpetitive games that the brighter pupil usually wins; such games should be balanced with others, like lotto, that are won almost by chance. If skill games are mixed with chance games, the slower pupils can sometimes win. Adults playing games with children—particularly in remedial situations—should usually contrive for the children to win.

BE A GOOD PHONICS EXAMPLE

Most teachers want to be good examples of standard speech for their students and a number of instructors may be concerned about the pronunciation to use in phonics lessons. A friend of the author's, coming from what is considered the "deep South," was made aware of some possible confusion in the giving of individual tests to midwestern students because her sound-symbol patterns were slightly different from that of the children she was testing. In contrast, a Minnesota-reared teacher might normally say "Market" with an audible /r/ and wonder how to pronounce the same word when teaching Philadelphia children the phonics for the name of their city's main street. Should she say something akin to "Mockett" or "Mahkut"? In other words, is there a guide for the correct phoneme that goes with its grapheme in the words used in phonics lessons?

Most teachers use an acceptable standard dialect and find little cause for undue concern, yet some thoughts and suggestions may be presented.

The most prevalent dialect in the United States is one that has been called Standard General American. It may also be nicknamed something like "network American" or "broadcast American" because General

American is the speech used on network radio and television and in most motion pictures. Since children in all parts of the country probably have been exposed to this predominant Standard General American dialect through these media, teachers who use it will cause little confusion. Teachers who speak Standard Eastern or Standard Southern dialects, however, may need to exercise special care if they are teaching in areas where other dialects are locally standard. They may adapt their enunciation of particular sounds. They may instead, or also, give their pupils time to become adjusted to the teacher's different dialect. They will find dictionaries useful guides for the Standard General American pronunciations.

Wherever they are teaching, teachers should accept the particular *standard* speech sounds of that area; in other words, a teacher who uses General American should accept standard Southern pronunciation from pupils in, say, Columbia, South Carolina. (But please note that word *standard*, because most communities do not wish to promote nonstandard dialects such as "hillbilly," "Brooklynese," and "border English.")

LINGUISTICS TRIES TO KEEP US PRECISE

Probably the most important contribution that the ongoing interest in linguistics has for the teacher of phonics and reading is that it helps make us more precise in our thinking about language. Linguists are constantly reminding teachers that the real language is oral speech and that the written word only represents that speech. Teachers of phonics need to keep in mind that letters merely represent sounds rather than "have a sound" or "make a sound" in themselves. Likewise, words were originally oral and the written words only stand for the spoken words.

Many teachers fully realize that letters of the alphabet do not in themselves have sounds, yet find it more convenient to say "the *t* sound" rather than the longer "the sound that we hear at the beginning of the word *take*" or "the sound we most often associate with this letter" (pointing to a *t*). But care is necessary in using this convenience, to assure that students understand the primacy of speech in reading and phonics instruction. Differentiating between letters and the sounds they represent is wise, to avoid confusion between the two.

In this book, the author has attempted to follow the rationale above, with the liberties taken done to avoid stilted, involved, or technical sentences or vocabulary. This intention is one reason for the phonics generalizations being phrased as they are.

5 The Vocabulary of Phonics

A specialized vocabulary is characteristic of every organized body of knowledge. Whether the subject is the stock market, basketball, or phonics, whoever works in it needs to know its particular terminology.

The terms, concepts, and examples in this chapter provide some of the background necessary for teaching phonics. Some have also been briefly or extensively explained in other parts of this book.

The terms are presented in this chapter in groups pertinent to several areas of knowledge, in alphabetical order within each group. The groups are:

> phonics terms
>
> structural analysis terms
>
> basic linguistics terms
>
> dictionary terms

Here is a list in a single alphabetical sequence:

Term	Group
accent	dictionary terms
affix	structural analysis
auditory discrimination	phonics
base word	structural analysis
consonant	phonics
consonant blend	phonics
consonant digraph	phonics

controller consonant	phonics
derivative	structural analysis
diacritical mark	dictionary terms
diphthong	phonics
final consonant	phonics
grapheme	basic linguistics
inflectional ending	structural analysis
initial consonant	phonics
linguistics	basic linguistics
meaning unit	structural analysis
medial consonant	phonics
morpheme	basic linguistics
phoneme	basic linguistics
phonics	basic linguistics
phonogram	basic linguistics
prefix	structural analysis
root	structural analysis
schwa	dictionary terms
stress	dictionary terms
suffix	structural analysis
syllabic consonant	phonics
syllable	structural analysis
visual discrimination	phonics
voiced and unvoiced consonant sounds	phonics
vowel	phonics
vowel digraph	phonics

PHONICS TERMS

The terms that follow are those most often used today in relation to phonics instruction by teacher's manuals, workbooks, tests, and phonics guide-books. An attempt has been made to include the more popular synonyms.

auditory discrimination.   The ability to distinguish sounds. Distinguishing between the sounds of a violin and a viola is an example of auditory discrimination. So is recognizing the difference between two vocalists on the radio. A child who recognizes the difference between the sounds of *pin-pen* or *bid-bit* has developed the ability to discriminate auditorily. We all learn to note the differences among sounds, and such a learning is, of course, indispensable to phonics instruction. Auditory discrimination is a psychological or mental factor; hearing (acuity) is physical. Compare **visual discrimination.**

consonant. A speech sound that is made by a blocking of outgoing air by a part of the mouth: also, a sound that is not a vowel; also, the letter(s) that represent(s) this kind of sound. Some consonant letters represent more than one consonant speech sound and some sounds are represented by more than one consonant letter or combination. The sounds associated with the underlined parts of the words in the following list are the 25 most commonly used consonant sounds in English. Some of these 25 sounds may also be represented by other letters, such as the letter *x*, but the underlined letters are those most often used.

boy	my	yellow
do	no	zone, boys
foot	pop	song
gay	run	chair
he	so, cent	shoe
wheat	toy	thin
joy, gem	very	them
kite, cake	walk	treasure
like		

A consonant may be specified by reference to its location in the word. Thus an *initial consonant* is one that begins a word—*baby*; a *medial consonant* is in the middle of a word—*later*; a *final consonant* is at the end of a word—*red*.

consonant blend. A quick sequence of consonant sounds represented by a group of two or more consonant letters; also called *consonant cluster* or *consonant sequence*. A consonant blend contains two or more consonant sounds that come in a fast succession in which they are partially merged or blended together, yet are still distinguishable. There is no vowel sound intervening between the consonant sounds of a consonant blend. The letters *l*, *r*, and *s* and the consonant digraphs (see the explanation that follows the list below) *sh* and *th* are common to many blends. A few of the very numerous consonant blends are illustrated by the underlined letters in this list:

> clear, blade; milk, film, health
> camp
> want, sink, science

d<u>r</u>y, bi<u>rd</u>; <u>p</u>ray, car<u>p</u>

ea<u>st</u>, eat<u>s</u>; ras<u>p</u>, lap<u>s</u>e

<u>sh</u>rink; mar<u>sh</u>

<u>tw</u>in, queen (*see the explanation that follows*)

<u>th</u>read; ear<u>th</u>

gli<u>mp</u>se

<u>s</u>pread

<u>str</u>ap

The last three words contain three-letter and three-sound consonant blends. Words like *thread, earth, shrink, marsh,* and *health* contain two-sound blends.

In *queen, quiet,* and the like, the letters *qu* represent the sound /kw/, which is a blend; in *technique,* the sound of the *qu* is /k/ and the *qu* is a consonant digraph; see the entry **consonant digraph.** The difference between a consonant blend and a consonant digraph is significant. In words like *green,* the letters *gr* represent a blend; the sounds /g/ and /r/ are merged or blended to form a sound /gr/ in which, nevertheless, the two sounds can be distinguished. By contrast, in words like *she,* the letters *sh* represent a single sound that is not separable; /s/ and /h/ cannot be distinguished; although we use the two letters for convenience, they form one sound which is sometimes represented as /ʃ/ to show that it is a simple single consonant. These two consonants as used to represent one sound are called a *consonant digraph.* The same term applies to the letters *th* in *thin* and *then*; the sound is not /t/ + /h/ but unvoiced /th/ in *thin* and voiced /th/ in *then*—not blends but single sounds that are sometimes rendered by [θ] and [ð].

A combination distinguished from a consonant blend is exemplified by the *bl* in *able, table, treble,* and the like or by the *dl* in *handle, needle*; the *er* or *re* of *theater, theatre* suggests something similar; so does the *(e)n* of *eaten, given, broken.* The kind of sound that these combinations represent is called a **syllabic consonant.** These *bl, dl,* and their likes are pronounced as syllables and some people hear a brief "uh" or /ə/ (schwa) sound in the syllable, whereas *bl* in *blow,* for a contrary example, does not represent a syllable. A teacher may need to be aware of this refinement even though there may not be a need to share it with pupils.

consonant digraph. Two side-by-side consonant letters that spell a single consonant sound. Among the familiar two-letter symbols that represent one speech sound (one phoneme) are these:

ch: rich, chocolate

sh: shoe, brush

gh: rough

ph: phone, graph

wh: who

th: there

th: thin

ng: sing

You will note that the two letters in these consonant digraphs represent a sound different from that which the individual or blended sounds of the digraph letters would represent. Thus *gh* and *ph* represent /f/, and *th* signifies either /th/ or /th/—respectively voiced as in th*en* or unvoiced as in th*in*.

The term *consonant digraph* may also include the common combinations in which two letters represent the sound of one of the letters. Among such combinations are *ck* as in ba*ck*, *sc* as in *sc*ience, *gh* as in *gh*ost.

Classifying combinations of consonant letters is in some cases difficult. To some ears, *nk* in th*ink* or th*ank* seems a digraph; others hear it as a blend of the /ŋ/ of *sing* with the familiar /k/ sound, and render the sound of *think* as /thiŋk/. Even more uncertain is the *ng* combination. In *sing* or *singer*, *ng* is a digraph representing a single sound /ŋ/. But in *angle* or *finger*, *ng* can be taken to represent /ŋ/ + /g/, two separate sounds in two separate syllables; dictionaries divide these words *an-gle* and *fin-ger*. A teacher should give thought to how far these refinements should be pursued with pupils.

Still other combinations that are sometimes digraphs and sometimes represent blends are *qu* and *wh*. The combination *qu* spells the blend /kw/ in *qu*iet or *qu*een; it represents the one sound /k/ in techni*qu*e, hence is a consonant digraph in this word. The combination *wh* represents the simple sound /h/ in *wh*o and *wh*ose, hence is a consonant digraph in such words. In the pronunciation of an increasing number of people, *wh* represents the single sound /w/; examples are *when* = /wen/; *what* = /wät/, *white* = /wīt/. In these pronunciations, *wh* is a consonant digraph. But in another pronunciation of the same words, *when* = /hwen/, *what* = /hwät/, and *white* = /hwīt/, and *wh* is these words is a blend of /h/ with /w/ in that order, or a "backward" consonant blend. You may find dictionaries that consider this same /hw/ sound a single simple sound comparable to /sh/ or /th/; in their hearing, then, *wh* is a digraph for this simple sound. Almost surely, the teacher in the early grades need not present the whole complexity to young pupils.

Consonant digraphs are also called *consonant speech sounds* and *two-letter consonant symbols* (or *sounds*).

controller consonant.   This term is utilized to call attention to vowel sounds before certain consonants, particularly the consonant *r*. You may also encounter equivalent convenience terms, such as "r-controlled words," "the strong r," and "r-words" to call special attention to vowel sounds before the *r* in words. Actually, nothing is being controlled; rather some vowel sounds simply do not occur before the *r* because they are very difficult to say before an *r*. The short vowels are considerably modified, with the *i* in birth, *e* in her, and *u* in curt all coming out with about the same sound. It is just not easy, for example, to say a clear "long a" /ā/ in words like bare, care, and dare. The vowel sounds that do come out before an *r* often are somewhere between their long and short sounds; in many other situations it is a schwa sound. The awareness of this phenomenon of varying vowel sounds before an *r* is one that a teacher can use to help pupils in reading the many words that present it.

Some other consonants have effects on vowels that precede them but these effects are less easily perceptible. Some phonics materials take note of these consonants, particularly *l* and *w*.

diphthong.   Two side-by-side vowel letters that represent a single blended sound, as *oi* in the word *oi*l. The two vowel sounds are pronounced in one syllable with the tongue gliding from one position to the other to make the blended sound. The diphthong, however, functions as one phoneme.

There are two much used diphthong sounds that are each spelled in two ways. The diphthong sound /oi/ is spelled both *oi* and *oy*, the *oy* especially but not only at the ends of words. The diphthong sound /ou/ is spelled both *ou* and *ow*. Some examples are:

ointment, oyster	house, how
toil, toy	out, owl
boil, boy	mouth, town
join, joy	foul, fowl

Although the fact is unimportant for teaching children phonics, it should be remarked that linguists say all the "long" sounds of American English vowels are diphthongs. "Dragging out" the long sound of any vowel will help demonstrate that it tends to be a diphthong. The sound of "long *i*" in particular is the diphthong sound /ài/ or /äi/ as in *like* and is comparable to /òi/, usually spelled *oi* as in *oil*.

Side-by-side vowel letters do not necessarily represent diphthongs. They may be **vowel digraphs** (see this entry).

final consonant. A consonant that ends a word—*red*. See also **consonant.**

initial consonant. A consonant that begins a word—b*aby*. See also **consonant.**

medial consonant. A consonant in the middle of a word—*later*. See also **consonant.**

syllabic consonant. A combination of consonants that forms a syllable. See **syllable** for an explanation.

visual discrimination. The ability to see differences among letters, words, signs, colors, shapes, etc. Distinguishing the difference between a 1972 and a 1974 Ford Mustang is an example of visual discrimination; so is noting the difference in appearance between the words *come-cone* and *boast-beast*. We *learn* to discriminate visually and this skill is an important prerequisite for phonics instruction and for learning to read. Visual discrimination is sometimes included in the term *visual perception*.

Visual *acuity* is the sharpness of the eyesight—the physical measure of the distance, the quickness, and the fineness of detail that a person can see. *Fusion* indicates how well the person's eyes work together. Our visual acuity and fusion are physical factors. In contrast to these, visual discrimination is learned; it is a psychological factor. Compare **auditory discrimination.**

voiced and unvoiced consonant sounds. Speech sounds made with the vocal cords vibrating are called voiced sounds. The sound /t/ associated with *t* in t*op* does not require use of the vocal cords and so is unvoiced; the sound /d/ of d*oll* is voiced. Making the sound /b/ of b*e* in isolation (voiced) and comparing it to the isolated sound /p/ of p*at* (unvoiced) helps the speaker to feel the difference in the throat.

Voiced consonants include the beginning sounds heard in b*ig*, d*og*, g*ot*, j*ug*, l*ady*, m*om*, n*o*, r*ug*, v*ast*, w*ish*, y*ell*, z*ip*.

Unvoiced consonants include the beginning sounds heard in p*al*, k*ind*, s*un*, t*op*, h*im*, f*un*.

The digraph *th* represents the two sounds /th̲/ and /th/; the first is voiced, the other unvoiced. In the word *that*, the *th* is voiced; in the word *thin*, the *th* is unvoiced. This difference can also be heard in *bathe*, where the sound is voiced, and *bath*, where it isn't. In dictionaries these two sounds associated with *th* are marked with different symbols to distinguish them (as /<u>th</u>/ and /th/ here). More examples of unvoiced th are *th*ink, tee*th*, clo*th*. Examples of voiced th are they, smoo*th*, fur*th*er, *th*ose.

vowel.   An unobstructed speech sound; that is, a sound uttered without friction and with a more or less open mouth; there is no blocking of outgoing air. There are 19 common sounds represented by the vowel letters *a*, *e*, *i*, *o*, *u*, *y*, and *w*. All vowels are voiced; that is, the vocal cords are used in making sounds represented by vowel letters.

vowel digraph.   A combination of two successive vowel letters that spells one sound (also called *adjacent vowels* or *vowel pair*). Such combinations include:

p<u>ai</u>n	sw<u>ea</u>t	f<u>oe</u>
g<u>au</u>ge	sh<u>ea</u>r	g<u>oo</u>d
<u>au</u>thor	<u>ee</u>l	br<u>oo</u>m
l<u>aw</u>n	b<u>ee</u>r	c<u>ou</u>gh
r<u>ay</u>	v<u>ei</u>n	c<u>ou</u>sin
p<u>ea</u>	y<u>ie</u>ld	b<u>ow</u>l
gr<u>ea</u>t	<u>oa</u>k	b<u>ui</u>ld

These combinations are not always digraphs. The vowel letters may be in different syllables and the sounds independently pronounced:

b<u>ea</u>tify	c<u>oe</u>rce
r<u>ee</u>nter	c<u>oe</u>xist
r<u>ei</u>nforce	c<u>oi</u>ncide
cl<u>ie</u>nt	c<u>oo</u>perate
b<u>oa</u>	c<u>oo</u>rdinate

Vowel digraphs differ from diphthongs (see **diphthong**) in that the digraph represents a single sound, as *ai* = /ā/ in *pain*, whereas the diphthong represents the "gliding" succession of two sounds, as *oi* = /ȯi/ in *toil*.

A number of practical generalizations may be taught to children about vowel digraphs; some are offered in Chapter 3.

Self Quiz 8

PHONICS TERMS

1. A lesson that emphasizes rhyming endings is a lesson that is attempting to develop: auditory acuity   auditory discrimination   visual perception   fusion.   Circle the answer.

2. Visual discrimination would be demonstrated by pupils' seeing differences between the word *got* and the word(s) _____ _____ .

3. *g i r l*   Circle the initial consonant.

    t o t a l   Circle the medial consonant.

    t r i p   Circle the final consonant.

4. In the word *clothes*, is there a consonant blend? If there is, write the letters that represent it: _____ .

5. *b r i g h t   s p r o u t   f l a s k   g r a s p*   In these four words, circle the letters representing consonant blends. Careful now, circle *all* consonant blends.

6. *t h i n g*   Does this word include a consonant digraph? If it does, circle the letters that represent the digraph(s).

7. *p h o n i c s   f l a s h   q u i c k   c h u n k   w h i c h*   In these five words, circle the letters that represent the consonant digraph(s). *All* of them.

8. Write a word that demonstrates the consonant that most strongly influences preceding vowels. Circle this "controller" letter.

9. *b a t h*   Circle all letters in this word that are voiced.

10. *t e e t h   t h e i r   b r o t h e r   t h i r d*   In these words, indicate the voiced *th* sound by circling the letters that represent them (not the unvoiced sounds).

11. Write one word that uses *y* to spell a vowel sound: _____

_____. Write another word that uses *w* to

spell a vowel sound: _____.

12. *pointing   count   tower   crow*   Circle *all* the diphthongs.

Answers follow Chapter 6.

STRUCTURAL ANALYSIS TERMS

Longer words are pronounced more efficiently by analyzing them for syllables and meaning units rather than by a labored letter-by-letter sounding approach. The terms discussed in this section help to explain structural analysis.

affix.   An inclusive term that means a prefix, a suffix, or an inflectional ending that is attached to a root or base word.

lonel<u>y</u>   <u>pre</u>pay<u>ment</u>

<u>un</u>like   pass<u>ed</u>

See the entires **prefix, suffix, inflectional ending.**

base word.   A basic meaning unit, a word from which other words are derived by the addition of prefixes, suffixes, or another base word. In simple word analysis base word is the same as root word. When distinguished from a root, it may be an independent word without a suffix, prefix, or other combining element. The unit *foot* in foot*ball*, *crow*foot, foot*ing*, or *fore*foot is a base word; the unit *ped(e)(i)* is a root in ped*al*, pede*strain*, pedi*cure*, *im*pede, or *centi*pede and is not an independent word. See also the entries **affix** and **root.**

derivative.   A word formed by adding a prefix, suffix, or both, to a base or root word. By such additions, a new word and a new meaning are obtained. These new words, using basic parts of the source word, are called *derivatives* or *derived forms.* By adding the prefix *un* to the root word *happy* we get a new word with a new meaning, *unhappy.* Examples of derivatives and their source words:

pay—<u>pre</u>pay, pay<u>ment</u>, <u>re</u>pay

grace—grace<u>ful</u>, <u>dis</u>grace, grace<u>fulness</u>

read—read<u>er</u>, unread<u>able</u>, <u>re</u>read

decent—<u>in</u>decent, decent<u>ly</u>, decent<u>ness</u>

The addition of a prefix or a morphological suffix to a base word usually brings about a derivative. An inflectional ending alone will not bring about a derivative (a new word with a different meaning from the original base)—rather it will form plurals, possessives, tenses, and other grammatical variants.

inflectional ending. A suffix that shows the change of form a word undergoes when indicating plurals (*papers*), possessives (*child*'s) past tense (*want*ed), comparisons (*sweet*er, *sweet*est, *soon*er, *soon*est), and third person singular (*he likes, she wishes, it is do*ing). The changed forms are *inflections*. Inflectional endings do not change the way a word is used in a sentence or the word's meaning and should be distinguished from derivational suffixes, which usually do. English has few inflectional endings in contrast to other languages such as Spanish or Polish.

Inflectional endings may be added to the basic word (roast*s*), to compounds (potroast*s*) and to derivatives (roaster*s*). Inflections may also be called *simple variants*.

meaning unit. A root word, a prefix, a suffix, or an inflectional ending. Every word is made up of one or more meaning units. Substituting, adding, or taking away a meaning unit from a word alters the word in some way. A meaning unit is a *morpheme*.

prefix. A meaning unit represented by a letter or group of letters put at the beginning of a word to change the base word's meaning or form a new word; a meaningful beginning attached to a root word. The prefix joins its meaning with that of the word to which it is attached. Thus, fastening the prefix *un* to the word *able* gives us a new word with a new meaning.

root. A basic or core meaning unit to which may be added prefixes, suffixes, inflectional endings, or other roots. A root may also be called a base. When root word is distinguished from a base word, the root would not form an independent word whereas the base word could stand alone as a word; see the entry *base word*. Published phonics materials may employ the terms *root, root word*, and *base word* as having the same or varying meanings.

suffix. A meaning unit attached to the end of a root or base word; an affix which unites its meaning or function with that of the root it is attached to. Suffixes are morphemes and modify the basic word in some way.

There are two types of suffixes. **Derivational morphological suffixes** change the original meaning of the base word (book-book*ing*) and

inflectional suffixes which, for example, merely make the root a plural (book-book<u>s</u>). In words like act<u>or</u>, speak<u>er</u>, rus<u>ty</u>, and friend<u>less</u>, the added endings are morphological suffixes which have created derivatives of the original base word and the meanings have been altered. In words like rock<u>s</u>, sweet<u>est</u>, Tom'<u>s</u>, and wash<u>ed</u>, the added endings are inflectional suffixes in which the base words have been varied only to the extent of indicating plural, comparison, possessive, and past tense. Linguists would say that derivational morphological suffixes change the form class (the way it is used in a sentence) of the base word whereas inflectional suffixes do not. See also, **derivative** and **inflectional ending.**

syllable.   A unit of speech sound. Usually it is a word or a word part that contains a vowel sound; however, the vowel sound may be only minimally present in a syllabic consonant (see below in this definition). The vowel sound may be the entire syllable, or may be associated with one or more consonant sounds.

In written or printed words, syllables may be recognized by visual analysis. A written or printed word usually represents as many syllables as it has vowel letters, vowel digraphs, or diphthongs (disregarding the final "silent" *e* in words like *gate*). Spoken syllables may not correspond to the word divisions in dictionaries or in writing—we say /'bil-diŋ/ but we write *build-ing*.

Some words contain syllables that have little or no vowel sound. In *bottle* = /'bät-ᵊl/, *eaten* = /'ēt-ᵊn/, or *botany* = /'bät-ᵊn-ē/, the /l/ and /n/ are called *syllabic consonants* because they have only the brief schwa sound /ᵊ/ in the syllables with them.

Self Quiz 9

STRUCTURAL ANALYSIS TERMS

1. How many meaning units are in *monthly?* _____

2. yes   no   In the word *impersonal*, are the number of meaning units and the number of syllables equal? Circle the answer.

3. *u n m a r k e d*   Circle all the affixes.

4. *carry brother colorful unending disheartened*
   Circle the root or base part of each word.

5. *ear faster prettiest striking manly lands foxes*
   Circle all likely inflectional endings.

6. Write a derivative of the word *fair:* _____.

7. *kindest girl's gladness hearty indoor* Circle the
   words that are likely derivatives.

Answers follow Chapter 6.

BASIC LINGUISTICS TERMS

Linguistics is an all-embracing word that refers to several approaches in the scientific study of language. Some of its branches are *phonetics, orthography, morphology, etymology,* and *semantics.*

Phonetics deals with the sounds of language. Orthography deals with spelling. Our subject, phonics, extends into both phonetics and orthography. *Etymology* concerns the origin and derivation of words—an aspect of historical linguistics. *Semantics* concerns meaning in language.

Linguists, those who work in the field of linguistics, are interested in the patterns and structures of language. Some linguists have devised methods and materials for teaching reading based on the word-structure and sentence-structure patterns of the English language.

grapheme. A written or printed letter or combination of letters that stands for a speech sound. A grapheme transcribes the sound; it is a "written-down" phoneme (see **phoneme**). In other words, the spelling of a speech sound is a grapheme.

The word *fat* has three graphemes, each grapheme representing a different sound (phoneme). The word *she* has two graphemes: a two-letter grapheme *sh* that shows the written spelling of the sound /sh/ and the one-letter grapheme *e* that is the written symbol for the second sound heard in the word, /ē/.

Since English does not have a one-to-one correspondence of phonemes with graphemes, a particular sound may be represented by different letters or letter combinations. Note the variety of graphemes that stand for the same phoneme (sound) in these examples:

shun, mission, nation, machine (phoneme /sh/)

neighbor, able, cafe, steak (phoneme /ā/)

A few words are written without graphemes for some sounds:

$$\text{rhythm} = /'\text{ri}\underline{\text{th}}\text{-əm}/$$

$$\text{enthusiasm} = /\text{in-'th(y)ü-zē-,az-əm}/$$

The schwa sound /ə/ in the syllable with /m/ in these words has no grapheme to represent it.

linguistics.   See the introductory explanation in this section.

morpheme.   A word or a word part that carries meaning. Base words, prefixes, suffixes, and inflectional grammatical endings are morphemes. In the makeup of the word *unthoughtful* there are three meaning units or morphemes: (1) *un*, (2) *thought*, (3) *ful*.

The base word *storm* is a meaning unit, or morpheme. *Stormy* has two morphemes, the base *storm* and the suffix *y*. *Stormdoors* has three morphemes—the base words *storm* and *door* and the grammatical ending (or inflection) *s*. Be careful—a syllable is not always a morpheme. *Window*, *little*, and *candy* each have two syllables, but each is only one meaning unit, thus one morpheme. Words like *workable*, *amoral*, *sensible* all have three syllables but only two meaning units or morphemes.

Morphemes that can be used as words, such as *order*, are "free" morphemes. Morphemes that are used only with others, such as *dis* and *ly* in *disorderly*, are "bound" morphemes.

phoneme.   A sound that is used in the speech of a particular language; the smallest bit of sound that distinguishes one word from another in that language. Phonemes—the atoms of language—are grouped to make words. The word *man* is made up of three phonemes or speech units: /m/a/n/. The word *chin* is also made up of three units of sound: /ch/i/n/. (In this book, /ch/ is considered one phoneme, in accordance with classroom orientation and with the phonics materials and the dictionaries used in schools. Linguists, however, are likely to discriminate two or more phonemes in /ch/.)

The human voice is capable of producing a variety of sounds. However, only about forty-four such sounds, or phonemes, are commonly used in saying standard American English words. These phonemes are represented by letters and combinations of letters, with many phonemes spelled more than one way.

consonant letters and consonant combinations	*t, sh, k, ck, f, ph, th,* etc.
vowel letters and vowel combinations	*a, oi, ai,* etc.

consonants and	}	*you, eigh, ough*
vowels in groups	}	(youth, eight, through

The written phoneme is a grapheme (see **grapheme**).

Stress may be a phoneme, but is not usually written in English (compare "get *up on* time" and "ride *upon* a horse") or is mingled with other phonemes (*desert* = /'dez-ərt/, /də-'zərt/). (If you know Spanish, you perceive the stress phoneme clearly distinguishing *esta* from *está*.)

phonics.   Knowledge about speech sounds and the symbols (letters) that represent the sounds; phonics is a way to analyze a printed word to arrive at the word's reading.

phonogram.   Commonly, a word part made up of a letter or group of letters. "Word families" and "family names" are terms that have been used for "phonograms" in the past. The groups *ick, ight, ook, alk, oud, ide, ing, alt, at* . . . are phonograms. *Note:* A few authors may use the term *phonogram* synonymously with *grapheme*, but this is not correct.

Self Quiz 10

LINGUISTICS TERMS

1. The word *dog* has how many phonemes? _____

2. How many phonemes has the word *scarf*? _____

3. The word *that* has how many phonemes? _____

4. How many phonemes are in the word *chief*? _____

5. The word *my* has how many graphemes? _____

6. How many graphemes are in the word *skill*? _____

7. yes   no   In the word *paper*, are the number of graphemes and the number of phonemes equal? Circle the answer.

8. yes   no   In the word *theme*, does the number of graphemes equal the number of phonemes? Circle the answer.

9. The word *sing* has how many morphemes? _____

10. How many graphemes are in the word *phone?* _____ _

11. *Singers* contains _____ morphemes?

12. There are _____ morphemes in *handshake*.

13. The word *terrifying* contains _____ morphemes.

14. Phonics understandings are drawn from what branch(es) of linguistics?

_____

15. yes   no   Is there a consistent one-to-one relationship of phonemes and graphemes in English? In other words, is a sound always represented by the same letter(s)? Circle the answer.

Answers follow Chapter 6.

A FEW IMPORTANT DICTIONARY TERMS

accent.   See **stress.**

diacritical mark.   A mark used, as in a dictionary, to indicate pronunciation. Since dictionaries differ in their ways of indicating pronunciation, the number of diacritical marks they use, and the meanings of the marks, a pupil must learn to interpret the pronunciation key of the particular dictionary that is in use.

The two diacritical marks probably most often seen used in schools are:

> breve   (˘)   A mark that indicates the "short" sound of a vowel as in bĕd, sĭt, băck, lŭck, gŏt. (In this book the breve is not used and "short" sounds are indicated by /a/, /e/, /i/, etc.

> macron   (¯)   A mark which is used to show the "long" sound of a vowel as in māke, hē, hōpe, rīde, ūse. The mark is also called a bar.

schwa.   The "neutral" vowel sound heard in many unstressed syllables is named a *schwa;* its phonetic symbol is /ə/. The schwa approximates an "uh" sound. In normal speech, the italicized vowel letters in the list below, all in unaccented syllables, have the schwa sound:

*a*bout, sof*a*, met*a*l

gard*e*n, probl*e*m, eag*e*r

or*i*gin, dom*i*nate, cand*i*date

f*o*rget, eb*o*ny, *o*ppose, lem*o*n

lot*u*s, rapt*u*re, foc*u*s, circ*u*s

Note that any vowel letter can represent the schwa sound.

A growing number of dictionaries, textbook glossaries, and teacher guides to school reading materials use the schwa symbol /ə/. Pupils must understand the schwa symbol and sound to use the pronunciation key of most dictionaries.

The acceptability of the schwa symbol in unstressed symbols is very wide. Moreover, there is a growing tendency for use of the schwa symbol for all /ú/ (or "short u") sounds whether stressed or not. This is particularly true for one-syllable words such as b*u*t, th*e*, and c*u*t where the vowel sounds are often marked as schwas.

stress. The relative loudness, strength, hardness, or volume with which a word or syllable is said; the prominence given to a syllable in a word, which makes it stand out audibly in relation to other syllables. The term *accent* is substantially synonymous.

Words of two or more syllables contain a syllable that is stressed— uttered with more force than the other syllable(s). There are differences in stress, hence the terms *primary stress, secondary stress,* and *unstressed.* Consider a four-syllable word:

gen-e-*ra*-tion	primary stress; loudest
gen-e-ra-tion	secondary stress; next loudest
gen-*e*-ra-*tion*	unstressed; least loud
/ˌjen-ə-ˈrā-shən/	pronunciation key with stress marks

Most words used in beginning reading instruction are made up of one or two syllables; for these, the teaching of stress is not necessary. The few longer words that children use have probably been heard and spoken by them many times (*grandmother; tomorrow; television,* which may be *'tele,vision* or *,tele'vision*). However, knowledge of stress is important in using a dictionary to learn a new word or in reading a word one has heard and knows orally but does not recognize by sight.

Children can be shown that a transfer of stress from one syllable to another can influence the form class and meaning of the word. An example is: "It's a *per*fect musical composition—it took time to per*fect* it." Other examples: *object, present, content.*

Self Quiz 11

REVIEW OF CHAPTER 5

Are you ready to take a short quiz on the vocabulary of phonics? See how you do on this selection of items from the entire chapter.

1. There are _____ phonemes in the word *father*.

2. *p h o t o g r a p h*   Circle each grapheme.

3. *r e f o r m s*   Circle the morphemes that make up the word.

4. *c h e s t   t r u c k   s m a l l*   Circle all the consonant blends.

5. *t h o u g h   c h u r c h   s h o u l d e r   w h i c h   l a u g h i n g*   Circle all the consonant digraphs.

6. In words such as *under*, *dirty*, and *ever*, the underlined vowels are influenced by ___ _ _____ .

7. Write two words, each word containing a different diphthong phoneme. _____

8. *c l e a r   c e r t a i n   b e c a u s e   m o u n t a i n   s t r e e t   p o e t*   Circle all the vowel digraphs.

9. Add an inflectional ending to these words:

    end_____

    fill_____

10. *a n o t h e r   c o m p a n y   p a t   w o m a n   b e a u t i f u l*   Mark the vowel letters likely to be pronounced as schwa.

Answers follow Chapter 6.

6 *An Inventory of Phonics Abilities*

An individual informal inventory of word-analysis abilities makes up the final section of this book. Using it as a diagnostic tool, a teacher may discover clues to the relative strengths and weaknesses in a pupil's phonics abilities.

The inventory is given individually to a pupil. It is untimed, and is called "informal" because it does not have statistical normative data. This check of phonics skills does not attempt to yield a specific grade or year placement—rather it may be used effectively to find out (with a minimum of the guessing typical of group paper-and-pencil tests) what exactly a particular boy or girl knows or doesn't know about word analysis. Teachers should be more interested in becoming aware of specific deficiencies of an individual child than whether the child is 1.8 or 2.1 on a scale. Such general placement scores may be obtained from most group reading tests.

There are many valuable uses for a word-analysis inventory: with children whose work-skills performance is erratic, at the beginning of a teaching term for some pupils, for the new pupil arriving without any records, before beginning remedial teaching, or as a check-up of recent instruction.

CRITERIA

Although the inventory is informal and teachers may wish to have higher standards, a 70-percent figure would usually be considered a passing mark for each pupil test. If there are ten items in a test and a pupil is successful in seven of ten items, then his working knowledge of the particular phonics principle is likely an effective one and he probably needs no special effort for correction. But, again, teachers may wish to note any errors for future instruction.

The inventory covers skills that are taught and largely mastered by the end of the fourth grade. At what grade or book level a particular phonics skill is taught varies considerably with each school's curriculum and each publisher's set of materials. The inventory, *generally*, will fit many sequence-of-skill arrangements of basal phonics programs and other special phonics materials. However, teachers may have to skip about to accommodate the particular teaching curriculum they follow. Teachers may wish to try pupils on skills that have not yet been taught in order to determine how well some skills have been learned unconsciously through wide reading.

TEACHER-PUPIL COLLABORATION

A spirit of teacher-pupil collaboration is highly desirable in taking a word-recognition inventory. It is often best to give the test when there is a degree of pleasant atmosphere between teacher and pupil—probably not on the first day of school for a transfer pupil, for example. Usually it is best to tell a pupil what the inventory is and that its intention is to help plan forthcoming instruction. He is encouraged to do his best and the teacher may wish to praise him for his patience and determination— whether he does well or poorly. Sometimes, pointing out the adventure of working with nonsense-type words may gain or keep greater concentration of effort. Should the pupil tire easily, the inventory may be administered in parts.

When the inventory—or chosen parts of the inventory—is finished, you may wish to share the results with the test taker, noting the strengths and weaknesses the test reveals. This procedure often removes the mystery and fear of testing and may elicit the child's cooperation to concentrate on those areas he now knows he needs to work on. If there are any weaknesses, you may note the one or two skills where effort should start rather than overwhelm a pupil with many deficiencies.

TEACHER DETACHMENT

Take care to be positive with a pupil taking the inventory yet not to give clues or attempt to teach any of the phonics principles while administering the test. You may encourage a pupil to do his best and tell him that he may not always know all the answers because he may not yet have been taught some of the things in the quiz. However, take care not to show any overt pleasure or disappointment with the quality of the test taker's performance.

ADAPTING THE INVENTORY

Those who administer the inventory may wish to add more items, modify some, or use only those tests that fit their particular need or sequence of skills.

You may find it more convenient in administering the inventory to have the words of appropriate tests typed on separate sheets of paper for the pupil to use while you use the copy in the book. Some tests require the pupil to listen only; these would not have to be placed on separate sheets.

In addition to the pupil copy, you may wish to make a master "ditto" of the test as it appears in the book so that you can mark the copy and keep it as a record of the pupil's progress.

FAMILIARITY WITH THE INVENTORY

Before you give the inventory tests, you should be familiar with them. Taking a test yourself is one simple—and perhaps revealing—way of becoming comfortable with it. You will soon find the simple procedures almost automatic.

EIGHTEEN TESTS FOR PUPILS

Pupil Test 1. Visual Discrimination

Ask the pupil to point out the word in each line that is different from the others in the line. You may wish to use a card or bookmark to keep the child's attention on the proper line.

1. one	one	someone	one	one
2. but	but	but	butter	but
3. came	can	came	came	came
4. air	fair	air	air	air
5. man	man	many	man	man
6. sing	wing	sing	sing	sing
7. cat	cat	cat	rat	cat
8. look	look	like	look	look
9. fate	fate	fate	fake	fate
10. than	than	than	thin	than

Number correct: _____   Percent correct: _____

Criterion: 7 of 10   Criterion: 70 percent

Pupil Test 2. Auditory Discrimination

Read each set of words and ask the pupil to listen and answer to "Which word sounds different?" or "What word doesn't rhyme?"

1. cook	clock	cook
2. make	take	take
3. try	my	free
4. ball	dog	fog
5. brain	drain	brick
6. wing	song	thing
7. gray	way	stop
8. black	game	tame
9. fan	ran	same
10. cut	bet	met

Number correct: _____   Percent correct: _____

Criterion: 7 of 10   Criterion: 70 percent

Pupil Test 3. Letters and Sounds

Pointing to the first letter, ask: "What sound do you think of when you see the letter?" Or, for the purpose of the test, ask the pupil for "the sound of the letter." If the pupil gives the letter names, repeat the directions and if needed, give an example or two by using letters in the test, even adding a short vowel sound after the sound of the consonants, as "buh," for the letter b. Accept either of the two sounds represented by c, s, and g, and any reasonable sound of the vowels and of x, q, and y. If all vowels are given their long sounds another sound may be asked for—"What other sound do you think of when you see this letter?" Criteria here may well be higher than 70 percent.

b	p	i	s	f	l	u	c	d
r	y	o	k	h	j	t	a	x
v	n	e	m	w	g	z	q	

Number correct: _____   Percent correct: _____

Criterion: _____ of 26   Criterion: _____ percent

Pupil Test 4. Initial Consonants

Say something like this: "Here are some groups of letters made up to look like words. Say them for me." Score only for the initial consonant sounding. However, you may wish to make a note as to how the vowel and the final consonant are sounded.

bem	lun	seb
dor	mub	tud
fum	nad	vip
hes	pid	wos
jom	rin	yeb
kam		zot

Number correct: _____

Criterion: 12 of 17

Percent correct: _____

Criterion: 70 percent

Pupil Test 5. Final Consonants

Say something like: "Here are some groups of letters that are made up to look like words. Read them for me." The inventory, generally, is cumulative; that is, the pupil now should pronounce both the beginning and the ending consonant sounds correctly. The vowel sound may be noted but does not affect the scoring.

1. neb	6. jip
2. rad	7. rom
3. sif	8. wen
4. kel	9. vox
5. het	10. mev

Number correct: _____

Criterion: 7 of 10

Percent correct: _____

Criterion: 70 percent

Pupil Test 6. Consonant Blends

Although in this test the blend parts are the most important, you may wish to take note of the correctness of other consonant sounds. In scoring, ignore the vowel sounds. If the pupil is unduly puzzled by items 14 to 16, where blends are in the final positions, give help with the beginning parts of the nonsense words.

1. blem	9. plop
2. clut	10. sned
3. flib	11. swip
4. slem	12. striv
5. fras	13. scrat
6. grib	14. bist
7. trag	15. rask
8. skon	16. risp

Number correct: _____   Percent correct: _____

Criterion: 12 of 16   Criterion: 75 percent

Pupil Test 7. Consonant Digraphs

Learning whether the pupil knows the consonant digraphs is the purpose of this test, although other consonant sounds may be noted. Disregard how the vowel sounds are made. In item 6, either /hwes/ or /wes/ is acceptable. You may give the child help in beginning words 7 to 10 if he is unduly puzzled by the change in the digraph's position.

1. shom	6. whes
2. chis	7. bish
3. phob	8. mick
4. thub	9. ting
5. quin	10. fank

Number correct: _____   Percent correct: _____

Criterion: 7 of 10   Criterion: 70 percent

Pupil Test 8. Long and Short Vowel Sounds—Auditory Discrimination

Tell the pupil you will read some real words and some made-up words with various vowel sounds. Ask the student to say whether the word you read has a long or short vowel sound. You may note any differences in accomplishment between real and nonsense words. (Item 9, *fly*, long *i*.)

1. so	8. sun	15. steeb
2. gay	9. fly	16. fam
3. bee	10. fit	17. fide
4. got	11. oam	18. pub
5. cut	12. nop	19. brit
6. cat	13. sem	20. ube
7. fine	14. tay	

Number correct: _____   Percent correct: _____

Criterion: 14 of 20   Criterion: 70 percent

Pupil Test 9. One-Syllable Closed-Syllable Words

Ask the pupil to read the words. The vowels should all have their short sounds, as in *at, met, sit, not, but*, and *hymn* (*y* = short *i*).

1. mil	8. mub
2. fam	9. ab
3. bev	10. isk
4. clob	11. ryb
5. rab	12. em
6. ib	13. sil
7. nes	

Number correct: _____   Percent correct: _____

Criterion: 9 of 13   Criterion: 69 percent

Pupil Test 10. Accented Open Syllables

Ask the pupil to read the made-up words. The first vowels should all have their long sounds. A puzzled child may be told that there are two syllables in items 7 to 10 and that the first syllable is to be stressed. If the pronunciation of the second syllable departs from the appropriate sound, this may be noted but not scored.

1. bo	5. mo
2. de	6. ta
3. bry	7. shi-lat
4. fe	8. na-don

9. u-ly   10. sti-ben

Number correct: _____   Percent correct: _____

Criterion: 7 of 10   Criterion: 70 percent

Pupil Test 11. Vowel Digraphs

Ask the pupil to read the made-up words. In items 1 to 6, the digraphs have the long sound of the first vowel letter. In items 7 and 8, the short sound /e/ may be accepted for the *ea*, or the student may be asked to try the word another way. Items 9 and 10 call for the /ò/ sound heard in *auto, awful*.

1. teel   6. breel
2. fain   7. feab
3. blay   8. meag
4. poad   9. baw
5. staim   10. aust

Number correct: _____   Percent correct: _____

Criterion: 7 of 10   Criterion: 70 percent

Pupil Test 12. Vowels before *r*

Ask the pupil to read the made-up words. The object of the test is to discover the ability of the pupil in sounding vowels before the *r*. Is there sensible versatility in varying the sound of the vowel before *r* or is there only one consistently used sound or one pattern for all the vowels, such as trying to make all of them long, short, or schwas. You may wish to accept a few reasonable alternatives to the expected vowel sounds.

1. tir   6. cor
2. cler   7. meer
3. mur   8. bir
4. lar   9. jur
5. dar   10. vare

Number correct: _____   Percent correct: _____

Criterion: 7 of 10   Criterion: 70 percent

Pupil Test 13. Vowel-Consonant-*E* in One-Syllable Words

Ask the pupil to read the made-up words. The long sound of the first vowel is what we are primarily listening for.

1. nate	6. ude	10. rame
2. dile	7. mide	11. bule
3. cote	8. feme	12. bole
4. shabe	9. stode	13. sike
5. styne		

Number correct: _____   Percent correct: _____

Criterion: 9 of 13   Criterion: 69 percent

Pupil Test 14. Diphthongs

In these one-syllable words only the diphthong /ȯi/ is correct where *oi* and *oy* are used. In the *ou* and *ow* words, either the diphthong /au̇/ or the long *o* sound, /ō/, is correct. You may wish to ask the child to try *ou* and *ow* words a second time if only /ō/ is given consistently; you might ask whether there is another sound that those two letters sometimes "make."

1. foi	6. toub
2. croy	7. fow
3. noid	8. mout
4. stoil	9. oud
5. moy	10. gow

Number correct: _____   Percent correct: _____

Criterion: 7 of 10   Criterion: 70 percent

Pupil Test 15. The Hard and Soft Sounds of *C* and *G*

Ask the pupil to read the made-up words. You may wish to pay special attention to item 8 and try additional nonsense or real *gi-* words to determine the child's flexibility in reading this combination, wherein *g* may have either the hard or soft sound.

1. cen	3. cag	5. coss
2. cym	4. civ	6. cul

7. fac	10. gos	12. gen
8. gib	11. gyp	13. gant
9. guv		

Number correct: _____   Percent correct: _____

Criterion: 9 of 13   Criterion: 69 percent

Pupil Test 16. Syllabication and Blending (First of Three Tests)

Ask the pupil to pronounce the groups of letters that look like words. Accept any reasonable pronunciation of the syllables—the purpose of this test is to appraise (1) the pupil's realization that there are two syllables; (2) his success in blending the two syllables together without much pausing between them. Other phonics weaknesses may be noted, however.

1. habber	6. kamton
2. rentir	7. damser
3. lacten	8. bactis
4. dapner	9. foppin
5. sommer	10. lirden

Number correct: _____   Percent correct: _____

Criterion: 7 of 10   Criterion: 70 percent

Pupil Test 17. Syllabication and Blending (Second of Three Tests)

Ask the pupil to pronounce the groups of letters that look like words. Recognizing that there are two syllables and blending them without too much pausing between syllables are the important skills here. Other phonics weaknesses, however, may be noted.

1. bosar	6. ludis
2. hogin	7. mimut
3. madet	8. pishot
4. nusig	9. fobis
5. tapod	10. sethin

Number correct: _____   Percent correct: _____

Criterion: 7 of 10   Criterion: 70 percent

Pupil Test 18. Syllabication and Blending (Third of Three Tests)

Ask the pupil to pronounce the groups of letters that look like words. Accept any reasonable pronunciation. Note primarily how the first syllable is blended with the consonant-plus-*le* sound of the second syllable.

1. takle	6. magle
2. hidle	7. sakle
3. pikle	8. fumle
4. duble	9. redle
5. hocle	10. dable

Number correct: _____   Percent correct: _____

Criterion: 7 of 10   Criterion: 70 percent

ANSWERS TO THE SELF QUIZZES

Self Quiz 1. Answers

1. yes	5. no	9. no
2. yes	6. yes	10. yes
3. yes	7. yes	
4. no	8. yes	

You probably did well—say, seven or eight correct out of the ten. Well, however you did this time, you will do better as you go along. But more important, you will understand the *why* of these answers as you go further in this book.

Self Quiz 2. Answers

1. yes	5. yes	9. yes
2. yes	6. no	10. no
3. yes	7. no	
4. yes	8. no	

Did you do well? Or did you find some difficulty in deciding whether particular sound associations were completely regular? You will discriminate even better as we go on.

Self Quiz 3. Answers

Answers are suggested, and a possible rationale is given for each. You may have other answers with equally good or better rationale.

1. yes. Few words begin with *x*; moreover, this word is long.
2. yes. Two each of *u*, *l*, and *e*—unusual.
3. yes. Long, hyphenated, five *t*'s, *i* at the end.
4. no. The shape is ordinary. |nerve|
5. no. The length and shape are common.
6. yes. A six-letter word does not often have five tall letters. |little|
7. yes. Four *e*'s.
8. no. Nothing unusual.
9. yes. Many "tails" below the line. |grumpy|
10. no. Nothing unusual.

Self-Quiz 4. Answers

Suggested answers are not meant to be absolute. Context clues and a dictionary could be used for checking all words.

1. phonics and context
2. sight—memory and/or configuration
3. phonics
4. phonics and context
5. dictionary, very likely, and sight—memory
6. structural analysis
7. structural analysis
8. sight word—memory
9. sight word—configuration
10. phonics and/or sight—configuration

Self Quiz 5. Answers

1. No. The *ch* usually stands for the sound heard in *cheese*, less frequently for the sound heard in *chaos*—infrequently for the /sh/ sound.
2. Yes. The *f* here represents the sound we most often associate with the grapheme *f*.

3. Yes. That *t* may represent a /sh/ sound in the middle of a word is a useful generalization.

4. Yes. The *s* at the beginnings of words usually represents the /s/ sound and often at the end of words the /z/ sound. These two examples follow useful generalizations.

5. Yes. *g* is "hard" except before *i*, *e*, and *y*.

6. Yes.

7. Yes.

8. Yes. The letter *c* represents the sound /s/ before *i*, *e*, and *y*; otherwise it represents /k/. In this example the two *c*'s conform to the usual pattern.

9. Yes. In this word the two *t*'s represent one sound, /t/. This is the usual sound relationship of double consonant letters.

10. No. In this compound word, *th* is not a consonant digraph, but two different letters with two different sounds. Here *t* ends one part of the compound word and *h* begins another.

Self Quiz 6. Answers

1. Yes. Open syllable; *a* is long.

2. Yes. Closed syllable; *i* is short.

3. Yes. Closed syllable; *a* is short. The sound of *y* will be a short *i* or a long *e*, depending on your dictionary. Both vowels follow useful generalizations.

4. Yes. Open syllable; *e* is long. The vowel digraph *ee* represents a long *e* sound. Both follow useful generalizations.

5. Yes. The vowel digraph *oa* is one of the vowel pairs that represents the long sound of the first vowel. The most common sound associated with the *oa* pair is a long *o*.

6. No. Here *ai* stands for the sound of short *e*, a most infrequent association. The vowel digraph *ai* here definitely does not follow a useful generalization.

7. Yes. The *ow* combination usually stands for either long *o* as in *grow* or for the diphthong in *gown*. Here *ow* is the diphthong /aủ/ and this either/or choice of sound association is useful vowel guidance.

8. No. In a final vowel-consonant-*e* the *o* would be long if it followed a useful generalization.

9. Yes. In final consonant-vowel-*e*, *a* is long. It is long here and follows a useful generalization.

10. Yes. There's no question about *ee*; the combination should be long because it is an open syllable and a legitimate "walking rule" example. The *a* here represents a schwa sound and would follow the expanded generalization.

Should you find that you want to review some parts of the section on vowels to check on any of your answers, you will find that a second reading will be helpful in remembering the useful vowel sound associations.

Self Quiz 7. Answers

The generalization on which the answer is based is given in the rationalization that follows it.

1. *dack*est.   A last syllable is usually not stressed, especially when it is an inflectional ending.

2. In *dog*. This is the regular sound of *d*.

3. Short, *a* here being the only vowel letter in a closed, stressed syllable.

4. Of /k/. Being a digraph, *ck* represents only one sound.

5. Schwa, most likely, since unstressed vowels tend to be schwas. If the syllable is enunciated very carefully, the *e* might have the short sound /i/.

6. The *st* represents an ending blend.

7. *precynthir*. Prefixes are usually syllables; dividing between consonant letters is usual, but the *th* is ordinarily not separated, being a digraph.

8. *precyn*thir. The stress usually falls within the base word or root and tends not to fall on the last syllable.

9. /s/; *s* in *son*. Before *e*, *i*, and *y*, the letter *c* usually has the /s/ sound.

10. Short *i*. In the middles of words, *y* usually has this sound.

11. Schwa, most likely, this is an example of a vowel sound before *r*.

12. *goungle*. Remember that *le* takes the consonant letter that precedes it—even the *g* of *ng*—and with this consonant forms a syllable.

13. *goung*l e. The stress does not fall on *le* endings and tends not to fall on final syllables.

14. Of *g* in *got*; before *a*, *o*, *u*, the letter *g* usually has the hard sound.

15. Diphthong, most likely. The *ou* would not be pronounced as a schwa because this syllable is accented. When it does not represent schwa, *ou* is most likely to have the diphthong sound as in *out*.

16. *disrotion*. Both *dis* and *tion* make separate syllables.

17. d i s(r o)t i o n. The stress usually falls within the root or the base word. It tends not to fall on final syllables and rarely falls on the ending *tion*.

18. Long *o*. Because the syllable is open and accented, the schwa sound is excluded.

19. Schwa. The vowel letter in most unaccented syllables is pronounced as schwa; *tion* is unaccented and therefore contains the schwa sound.

20. (e x)(t o m e). Two syllables—there are two vowel letters plus one silent *e*. The separation is between the prefix and the base word or root.

21. e x(t o m e). The stress usually falls on the root or the base word rather than on a prefix; here, being a root or a base word outweighs being the last syllable.

22. The *o* is long. The letter *o* should have its long sound since it is in a final vowel-consonant-*e* and also since it is in the stressed syllable. In an unstressed syllable it might be pronounced as schwa.

23. The *s* has the sound of /z/; at the ends of words, *s* often represents this /z/ sound.

24. One syllable. The *ay* is a vowel combination or digraph, and has one sound. Since there is one vowel sound, there is one syllable.

25. Long *e*. The double letter *ee* usually has the long sound of *e*.

26. (s a)t e r. Here the *t* would probably be included in the second syllable, but either division or reading would be possible.

Self Quizzes 8, 9, 10, and 11, which appear in Chapter 5, will provide much additional practice with phonics terms and generalizations.

Self Quiz 8. Answers

1. auditory discrimination.

2. Any words similar in shape and letters used, as *get, gem, jot, pot.*

3. (g)i r l   (t)o t a l   t r i(p)

4. *cl* represents the blend in *clothes.*

5. (br)i g ht   (s pr)o u t   (fl)a(sk)   (gr)a(s p)

6. (t h)i(n g)

7. (ph)o n i c s   f l a(s h)   q u i(c k)(see note)(c h)u(n k)(see note)(w h)i(c h)
   Note: Here *qu* represents the blend /kw/; in a word like *technique* it would be a digraph. If you consider *nk* in *chunk* a diagraph or diagraph-blend, you would circle it too.

8. The "controller" letter is *r*.

9. b̶a̶t h. The /b/ sound is voiced; all vowels are voiced; /th/ here is not voiced—it is voiced in *bathe*.

10. t h̶e i r b r o t h̶e r

11. In *baby*, *style*, or *cry*, the letter *y* is a vowel letter. In *cow*, *owl*, or *town*, the letter *w* is a vowel letter.

12. p o i n̶t i n g c o̶ u̶n t t o̶ w̶e r There is no diphthong in *crow*.

The twelve questions require about 40 decisions. How did you do? Perhaps you discovered that your knowledge is not really as usable as you would like and that you need a second reading or more care in taking the quizzes.

Self Quiz 9. Answers

1. Two meaning units: the root *month* and the suffix *ly*.

2. No. Three meaning units: *im + person + al*. Four syllables: *im-per-son-al*.

3. u n̶m a r k̶e d̶ The *un* is a prefix; the *ed* is a suffix.

4. c̶a r r y̶ b̶r o t h e r̶ c̶o l o r̶ful un̶e n d̶i ng dis̶h e a r t̶e n e d

5. ear fast̶e r̶ pretti̶e s t̶ strik̶i n g̶ manly land̶s̶ fox̶e s̶
   There are no inflections in *ear*. There are none in *manly*; *ly* is a derivational suffix and changes the word from a noun to an adjective, whereas inflections do not change the word's meaning or change the way it is used in a sentence.

6. Possibilities include *fairly, unfair, fairminded, fairness, fairway*. Not *faired, fairs, fairing*.

7. k i n d e s t g i r l ' s g̶l a d n e s s̶ h̶e a r t y̶ i̶n d o o r̶ *Kindest* is not a derivative; it is an inflection. *Girl's* is an inflection. *Gladness* and *hearty* are derivatives of *glad* and *heart*. *Indoor* is a derivative of *door* by reason of the prefix *in*.

There were 24 decisions to be made in this self quiz. How did you do? One of the most difficult decisions to make is that between derivatives and inflections. Is a short review in order for you?

Self Quiz 10. Answers

1. Three phonemes: /d/ + /o/ + /g/.

2. Five phonemes: /s/ + /k/ + /ä/ + /r/ + /f/.

3. Three phonemes: /th/ + /a/ + /t/. The digraph *th* represents the single phoneme /th/.

4. Three phonemes: /ch/ + /ē/ + /f/. The digraphs *ch* and *ie* represent single phonemes.

5. Two graphemes: *m* + *y*.

6. Four graphemes: *s* + *k* + *i* + *ll*.

7. Yes. The five phonemes /p/ + /ā/ + /p/ + /ə/ + /r/ are represented by the five graphemes *p-a-p-e-r*.

8. Yes—three of each. There will *usually* be an equal number of graphemes and phonemes. Here /th/ + /ē/ + /m/ is represented by *th* + *e-e* + *m*. The /th/ and *th* correspond, as do the /m/ and *m*. The /ē/ is represented by the grapheme *e-e*; the final *e* is part of this grapheme because it indicates that the phoneme preceding /m/ is /ē/, not /ĕ/ as it would be if the word were *them* rather than *theme*.

9. One; *sing* is one meaning unit.

10. Three graphemes: *ph*, *o-e* which includes the final *e*, and *n*.

11. Three morphemes: *sing* + *er* + *s*. Each is a meaning unit that changes the word in some way.

12. Two morphemes: *hand* + *shake*.

13. Two morphemes: *terrify* + *ing*. (If you answered "Three" *and* see them as *terr(or)* + *ify* + *ing*, you were also correct.)

14. Phonetics. Phonics subject matter also extends into orthography.

15. No. Several graphemes may represent a particular phoneme (sound). Observe the different graphemes that represent the phoneme /k/: *court*, *choir*, *keg*, *technique*, *tack*.

Self Quiz 11. Answers

1. Five phonemes: /f/ä/th/ə/r/.

2. (p h o t o g r a p h) Eight graphemes (also eight phonemes).

3. (r e f o r m s) Three morphemes.

4. c h e (s t) (t r) u c k (s m) a l l

5. (t h) o u g h   (c h) u r (c h)   (s h) o u l d e r   (w h) i (c h)   l a u (g h) i (n g) (In *which*, the *wh* represents the blend /hw/; it is at the same time a digraph since the blend-sound sequence does not correspond to the letter sequence. It is also digraph if *which* is pronounced /wich/.

6. the "strong" *r*; the controller consonant *r*.

7. The words must have sounds like those you hear in *soil-toy* and *shout-clown*. These are the two most used diphthongs, with four spellings: *oi-oy* and *ou-ow*.

8. cl(ea)r cert(ai)n bec(au)se mount(ai)n (here *ou* is a diphthong) str(ee)t poet (this *oe* represents two vowel sounds; it is neither a digraph nor a diphthong).

9. Possibilities are: end*s*, end*ing*, end*ed*; fill*s*, fill*ed*, fill*ing*.

10. (a)noth(e)r comp(a)ny pat wom(a)n beaut(i)f(u)l or beautif(u)l.

SOME PRONUNCIATION SYMBOLS

/ə/ balloon, marine, collar, rival; verb, berth, over; bird, birth, pencil; come, work, sector; us, minus, sum, quorum; myrrh, myrtle; hearse; rough

/ᵊ/ bottle, kitten

/a/ bad; half (*but see also* /à/)

/ā/ made, aim, day, break, vein

/ä/ what, got; father (*but see also* /à/)

/à/ half, calf (*but see also* /a/); father (*but see also* /ä/)

/e/ net, tell

/ē/ be, me, beet, meat, sunny, money

/i/ lip, swim, syllable

/ī/ wide, sight

/ō/ go, dough, snow, lone

/ò/ all, raw, talk, cough, off

/ù/ bull, hood, good

/ü/ brute, food, through, threw, who

/aù/ out, now, bough

/òi/ boy, soil

/b/ baby, robe

/ch/ charm, reach, hatch

/d/ dim, mid

/f/ deaf, feed, photo, trophy, rough

/g/ gas, grass, wig, lag

/h/	hot, behold, whole
ıw/	what, when (*but see also* /w/)
/j/	join, gem, margin, lodge
/k/	keg, cap, core, fiscal, creek, track, sac, ache, Christian
/l/	luck, bulk, all, sole, soul
'm/	must, stem
/n/	near, earn
/ŋ/	ring, thong, angle, bank, ankle
/p/	pale, slip, copper
/r/	roll, or
/s/	sent, scent, cent, horse, place
ıh/	share, rash, machine, mission, ocean, lotion, physician
/t/	tame, ate
:h/	thumb, moth
:h/	these, seethe
ıv/	value, of, over
w/	wait, reward; (*and see also* /hw/) what, when
ıy/	year, beyond; unit = /'yü-nət/, beauty = /'byü-tē/
/z/	zeal, breeze, razor, toes, rose, present
:h/	azure, pleasure, invasion

/ /	Symbols enclosed between these pairs of lines represent sounds rather than alphabet letters, as /'āl/ = *ale*, /'āt/ = *eight*.
'	This mark precedes the syllable that has primary or strongest stress, as /'bās/ = *base*, /ə-'bās/ = *abase*.
,	This mark precedes the syllable that has secondary or next-strongest stress, as /ə-'brē-vē-ˌāt/ = *abbreviate*.
–	This hyphen shows the separation between syllables as sounded; it may not coincide with the separation between parts of the word as written or printed; thus /'fen-dər/ is divided *fend-er* at the end of a line.

Index